THE AUSTRALIAN
Women's Weekly

FAST
vegies

acp
books

contents

With the exception of roasted root vegetables, which can take a long time to cook, vegetables benefit from quick cooking – it helps them retain their colour, flavour and nutrients. One of the easiest ways to cook vegetables fast is in the microwave. Place in a microwave-safe dish with a small amount of water and cover with a plate. Cook on high (100%). Test them just before they're ready – you can always cook them a little longer. Drain immediately. Don't leave them sitting in their cooking water as they will quickly lose their colour. If not served immediately, rinse with cold water to stop any further cooking and to retain their bright colour – when you reheat briefly just before serving, you can do so with no ill effects. If you're going to pan-fry or roast potatoes for one or two people, cook them first in the microwave. Cut potatoes into pieces and microwave in a covered bowl with a little water on high (100%) until just tender. Drain immediately and cover the bowl with a hand towel to absorb excess moisture. Rough up the outside of the potato with a fork, then add to a heated oiled frying pan or oven dish. It won't take long at all for the outside to brown and crisp, and the insides will be deliciously floury.

finger food

Onion and zucchini fritters

1 cup (150g) besan flour
2 cloves garlic, crushed
1 teaspoon chilli powder
¼ teaspoon ground turmeric
2 teaspoons salt
⅓ cup (80ml) water, approximately
1 medium white onion (150g), sliced thinly
8 green onions (200g), sliced
½ cup loosely packed fresh coriander leaves
2 medium zucchini (240g), grated coarsely
vegetable oil, for deep-frying

1 Sift flour into medium bowl; add garlic, chilli, turmeric and salt.
Whisk in enough of the water to form a smooth paste.
2 Add both onions, coriander and zucchini; mix well.
3 Heat oil in wok or large saucepan; deep-fry level tablespoons of
mixture, in batches, until fritters are browned. Drain on absorbent paper.

on the table in 35 minutes
makes 24 **per fritter** 2.1g total fat (0.3g saturated fat); 180kJ (43 cal);
2.2g carbohydrate; 3.2g protein; 1.3g fibre

Sumac wedges

Sumac, a granular spice ranging in colour from a deep terracotta to almost-black purple, is used extensively from the eastern Mediterranean through to Pakistan. Both in cooking and as a condiment, sumac's tart astringency adds a delightful piquancy to food without the heat of a chilli.

1kg potatoes, washed
2 tablespoons sumac
2 tablespoons olive oil

1 Preheat oven to 240°C/220°C fan-forced. Lightly oil oven tray.
2 Cut potatoes into wedges; combine in large microwave-safe bowl with sumac and oil.
3 Cook, covered, in microwave oven, on high (100%), for 5 minutes.
4 Place wedges, in single layer, on tray. Roast, uncovered, 20 minutes or until wedges are crisp. Sprinkle with sea salt flakes, if desired.

on the table in 30 minutes
serves 4 **per serving** 9.3g total fat (1.3g saturated fat); 949kJ (227 cal); 28.1g carbohydrate; 5.1g protein; 4.3g fibre

Mini zucchini frittatas

You will need four 12-hole non-stick mini (1 tablespoon/20ml) muffin pans for this recipe. If you do not own that many, make frittatas in batches, placing the cooked ones on a wire rack while you bake the remainder.

8 eggs
1 cup (240g) sour cream
¼ cup finely chopped fresh chives
1 large yellow zucchini (150g), grated coarsely
1 large green zucchini (150g), grated coarsely
⅓ cup (25g) finely grated parmesan cheese
2 tablespoons chopped fresh chives, extra

1 Preheat oven to 180°C/160°C fan-forced. Oil four 12-hole mini (1 tablespoon/20ml) muffin pans.
2 Whisk eggs with two-thirds of the sour cream in large bowl until smooth; stir in chives, zucchini and cheese.
3 Divide mixture among holes of pans. Bake, uncovered, 15 minutes; turn onto wire rack to cool.
4 Top frittatas with remaining sour cream and extra chives. Serve at room temperature.

on the table in 35 minutes
makes 48 **per frittata** 3.0 total fat (1.7g saturated fat); 142kJ (34 cal); 0.3g carbohydrate; 1.5g protein; 0.1g fibre

Tomato chilli salsa

The tomato chilli salsa can be used as a dip with vegetables and corn chips or bread; or serve with grilled meat, fish, chicken or vegetables.

2 teaspoons vegetable oil
1 small red onion (100g), chopped finely
1 fresh small red thai chilli, chopped finely
1 clove garlic, crushed
1 small green capsicum (150g), chopped finely
400g can tomatoes
1 tablespoon finely chopped fresh coriander

1 Heat oil in medium frying pan, add onion, chilli, garlic and capsicum; cook, stirring, until onion is soft.
2 Add undrained, crushed tomatoes and bring to a boil, simmer, uncovered, stirring occasionally about 5 minutes or until mixture thickens slightly.
3 Transfer mixture to heatproof bowl and refrigerate 20 minutes.
4 Stir in coriander before serving.

on the table in 35 minutes
makes 1½ cups **per tablespoon** 0.6g total fat (0.1g saturated fat); 50kJ (12 cal); 1.2g carbohydrate; 0.4g protein; 0.4g fibre

Leek and fetta triangles

100g butter
2 cloves garlic, crushed
2 medium leeks (700g), sliced thinly
1 tablespoon caraway seeds
150g fetta cheese, chopped coarsely
⅓ cup (40g) coarsely grated cheddar cheese
4 sheets fillo pastry
2 teaspoons sesame seeds

1 Heat half of the butter in large frying pan, add garlic and leek; cook, stirring occasionally, until leek softens. Stir in caraway seeds; cook, stirring, 2 minutes.
2 Combine leek mixture in medium bowl with cheeses.
3 Preheat oven to 200°C/180°C fan-forced. Lightly oil oven tray.
4 Melt remaining butter in small saucepan. Brush one sheet of the fillo lightly with butter; fold in half lengthways. Place ¼ of the leek mixture at bottom of one narrow edge of fillo, leaving a 1cm border. Fold opposite corner of fillo diagonally across the filling to form a triangle; continue folding to end of fillo, retaining triangular shape. Place on tray, seam-side down; repeat with remaining ingredients to make four triangles in total.
5 Brush triangles with butter; sprinkle with sesame seeds. Bake, uncovered, about 10 minutes or until browned lightly.

on the table in 30 minutes
serves 4 **per serving** 34.2g total fat (21.6g saturated fat); 1772kJ (424 cal); 14.5g carbohydrate; 13.6g protein; 3.9g fibre

Frittata with two toppings

Frittata can be made several hours ahead and served cold or at room temperature.

2 tablespoons olive oil
1 medium white onion (150g), chopped finely
2 tablespoons finely chopped fresh flat-leaf parsley
2 tablespoons finely grated parmesan cheese
10 eggs, beaten lightly
20g butter
2 cloves garlic, crushed
8 button mushrooms
4 char-grilled artichokes, halved
¼ cup (50g) char-grilled capsicum, sliced thinly

1 Heat oil in medium frying pan; cook onion, stirring, until soft. Stir in half of the parsley.
2 Add cheese to the egg; pour into pan. Cook over a low heat, covered loosely, without stirring, about 8 minutes or until edges are set.
3 Cover pan handle with foil; place pan under hot grill until browned lightly and just set. Invert onto board.
4 Meanwhile, heat butter in small frying pan, add garlic and mushrooms; cook, stirring, until just tender. Stir in remaining parsley.
5 Cut frittata into 16 wedges, arrange on serving platter. Top half the wedges with mushrooms and half with artichokes and capsicum.

on the table in 35 minutes
serves 8 **per serving** 9.9g total fat (4.4g saturated fat); 736kJ (176 cal); 1.9g carbohydrate; 9.9g protein; 0.7g fibre

Beetroot dip

2 medium beetroots (320g), peeled, grated finely
⅓ cup (80g) sour cream
1 teaspoon red wine vinegar

1 Combine beetroot, sour cream and vinegar in small bowl.

on the table in 10 minutes
makes 1 cup **per tablespoon** 2.7g total fat (1.7g saturated fat); 150kJ
(36 cal); 2.2g carbohydrate; 0.6g protein; 0.7g fibre

Goat cheese and potato fritters

600g potatoes, peeled
¼ cup (60ml) cream
¼ teaspoon ground nutmeg
3 eggs, beaten lightly
2 egg yolks, beaten lightly
½ cup (75g) plain flour
250g firm goat cheese, crumbled
2 tablespoons finely chopped fresh flat-leaf parsley
pinch cayenne pepper
vegetable oil, for deep-frying

1 Boil, steam or microwave potatoes until tender; drain.
2 Mash potatoes in large bowl with cream and nutmeg until smooth. Add egg and egg yolk; beat until smooth. Stir in flour, cheese, parsley and cayenne pepper.
3 Heat oil in wok; deep-fry level tablespoons of the potato mixture, in batches, until fritters are browned. Drain on absorbent paper.

on the table in 35 minutes
makes 32 **per fritter** 5.1 total fat (1.9g saturated fat); 318kJ (76 cal); 4.6g carbohydrate; 2.6g protein; 0.4g fibre

25

Tomato and marinated bocconcini skewers

⅓ cup (80ml) olive oil
2 tablespoons balsamic vinegar
1 tablespoon finely shredded fresh basil
16 (150g) baby bocconcini cheese
16 baby rocket leaves
8 cherry tomatoes, halved

1 Combine oil, vinegar and basil in medium bowl; add cheese, toss to coat in marinade. Cover; refrigerate for 20 minutes.
2 Drain cheese; discard marinade. Wrap rocket leaves around cheese, then thread onto toothpicks with tomato.

on the table in 35 minutes
makes 16 **per serving** 6.0g total fat (1.6g saturated fat); 255kJ (61 cal); 0.2g carbohydrate; 1.7g protein; 0.2g fibre

Vegetable tempura with wasabi aïoli

2 medium carrots (240g)
1 medium red capsicum (200g)
1 medium green capsicum (200g)
1 large brown onion (200g)
2 egg whites
1 cup (150g) plain flour
½ cup (75g) cornflour
1¼ cups (310ml) iced water
vegetable oil, for deep-frying
800g butternut pumpkin, sliced thinly
400g broccolini
½ cup (125ml) soy sauce
wasabi aïoli
2 egg yolks
1 tablespoon lemon juice
1 tablespoon wasabi
1 clove garlic, quartered
½ cup (125ml) vegetable oil
1 tablespoon hot water

1 Using a vegetable peeler, cut carrots into long thin ribbons. Halve capsicums; discard seeds and membranes. Cut capsicum into 2cm-thick slices. Cut onion into thin wedges.
2 Make wasabi aïoli.
3 Just before serving, whisk egg whites in small bowl until soft peaks form. Sift flours into large bowl. Stir in the water; fold in egg white.
4 Heat oil in wok. Dip vegetables, one piece at a time, in batter; deep-fry, in batches, until browned lightly and crisp. Drain on absorbent paper; keep each batch warm as you deep-fry remainder.
5 Serve tempura with separate bowls of soy sauce and wasabi aïoli.
wasabi aïoli blend or process egg yolks, juice, wasabi and garlic until smooth. With motor operating, add oil gradually in thin stream; process until mixture thickens. Thin aïoli with the hot water, if desired.

on the table in 30 minutes
serves 6 **per serving** 34.4g total fat (4.9g saturated fat); 2295kJ (549 cal); 43.4g carbohydrate; 13.2g protein; 7.2g fibre
tips tempura batter must be made just before required. Do not overmix the batter – it should be lumpy.

Noodle and vegetable rolls

60g rice vermicelli noodles
½ medium carrot (60g), grated coarsely
½ small wombok (350g), shredded finely
1 tablespoon fish sauce
1 tablespoon brown sugar
¼ cup (60ml) lemon juice
12 x 17cm-square rice paper sheets
12 large fresh mint leaves
sweet chilli dipping sauce
¼ cup (60ml) sweet chilli sauce
1 tablespoon fish sauce
1 tablespoon lime juice

1 Place noodles in medium heatproof bowl, cover with boiling water; stand until just tender, drain. Using kitchen scissors, cut noodles into random lengths.
2 Place noodles in medium bowl with carrot, wombok, fish sauce, sugar and juice; toss gently to combine.
3 To assemble rolls, place 1 sheet of rice paper in medium bowl of warm water until just softened. Lift sheet carefully from water; place, with one point of the square sheet facing you, on board covered with tea towel. Place a little of the vegetable filling and one mint leaf vertically along centre of sheet; fold top and bottom corners over filling then roll sheet from side to side to enclose filling. Repeat with remaining rice paper sheets, vegetable filling and mint leaves.
4 Make sweet chilli dipping sauce.
5 Serve rolls with dipping sauce.
sweet chilli dipping sauce combine ingredients in small bowl.

on the table in 25 minutes
makes 12 rolls **per roll** 0.4g total fat (0.1g saturated fat); 205kJ (49 cal); 9.2g carbohydrate; 1.4g protein; 1.3g fibre

Roasted capsicums

2 medium yellow capsicums (400g)
2 medium red capsicums (400g)
¼ cup (60ml) olive oil
1 clove garlic, sliced thinly
1 tablespoon finely chopped fresh flat-leaf parsley

1 Quarter capsicums; remove seeds and membranes. Roast capsicum under grill or in very hot oven, skin-side up, until skin blisters and blackens. Cover with plastic or paper 5 minutes. Peel away skin; cut capsicum into thick strips.
2 Combine capsicum with remaining ingredients in medium bowl; thread onto skewers.

on the table in 20 minutes
serves 4 **per serving** 13.9g total fat (1.9g saturated fat); 660kJ (158 cal); 5.3g carbohydrate; 2.6g protein; 1.9g fibre

Fennel fritters

1 tablespoon finely chopped fresh fennel
1 medium fennel bulb (500g), chopped finely
3 green onions, chopped finely
1 small carrot (70g), grated finely
2 eggs, beaten lightly
75g ricotta cheese
¼ cup (35g) plain flour
2 teaspoons baking powder
vegetable oil, for shallow-frying

1 Combine fennel leaves and bulb, onion, carrot, egg, cheese, flour and baking powder in medium bowl; mix well.
2 Heat oil in large frying pan; shallow-fry heaped tablespoons of mixture until golden brown both sides and cooked through. Flatten slightly during cooking; drain on absorbent paper.

on the table in 35 minutes
makes 16 **per fritter** 3.2g total fat (0.8g saturated fat); 201kJ (48 cal); 2.7g carbohydrate; 1.8g protein; 0.7g fibre

Carrot and zucchini noodle rolls

You will need about 2 medium carrots (240g) and 3 small zucchini (270g) for this recipe.

1 cup coarsely grated carrot
1⅓ cups coarsely grated zucchini
2 green onions, chopped finely
1 tablespoon light soy sauce
1 tablespoon sweet chilli sauce
½ teaspoon sesame oil
1cm piece fresh ginger (5g), grated
8 x 22cm rice paper sheets

1 Combine carrot, zucchini, onion, sauces, oil and ginger in medium bowl.
2 To assemble rolls, place 1 sheet of rice paper in medium bowl of warm water until softened slightly. Lift sheet carefully from water, place on board; pat dry with absorbent paper.
3 Divide carrot mixture into eight portions; place one portion in centre of rice paper sheet. Roll to enclose filling, folding in sides after first complete turn of the roll. Repeat with remaining rice sheets and filling.

on the table in 20 minutes
serves 4 **per serving** 1.2g total fat (0.2g saturated fat); 318kJ (76 cal); 11.8g carbohydrate; 2.7g protein; 3.4g fibre
tip you can also use fresh rice noodle sheets, cut into 14cm x 16cm rectangles, to enclose the filling.

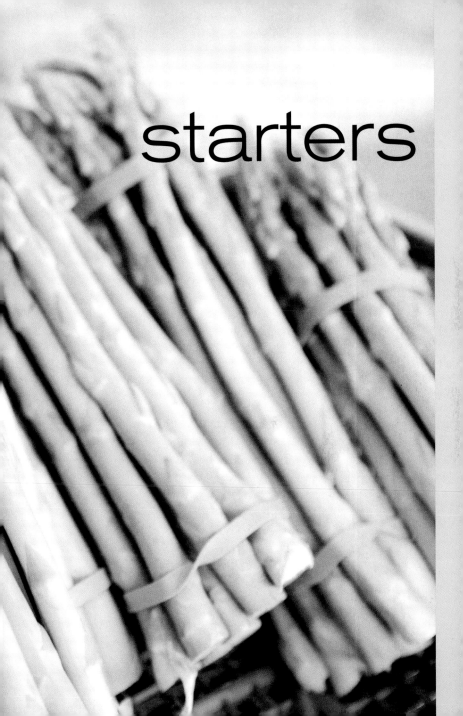

starters

Ham and asparagus spears with rocket salad

240g thinly sliced ham, halved
400g asparagus, trimmed
125g baby rocket leaves
250g yellow teardrop tomatoes, halved
2 tablespoons fresh baby basil leaves
¼ cup (20g) shaved parmesan cheese
dressing
2 tablespoons balsamic vinegar
2 tablespoons olive oil

1 Wrap ham around two asparagus spears; secure with toothpicks.
Cook on heated oiled grill plate (or grill or barbecue) until browned.
2 Make dressing.
3 Divide rocket, tomato and basil among serving plates. Drizzle with dressing; top with cheese.
4 Remove and discard toothpicks from asparagus. Serve asparagus with salad.
dressing place ingredients in screw-top jar; shake well.

on the table in 20 minutes
serves 4 **per serving** 13.3g total fat (3.1g saturated fat); 928kJ (222 cal); 9.1g carbohydrate; 16.4g protein; 2.6g fibre

Free-form spinach and ricotta pie

200g baby spinach leaves
2 tablespoons olive oil
1 medium brown onion (150g), chopped coarsely
1 clove garlic, crushed
2 teaspoons finely grated lemon rind
¼ cup coarsely chopped fresh flat-leaf parsley
2 tablespoons coarsely chopped fresh mint
1½ cups (300g) ricotta cheese
2 sheets ready-rolled puff pastry

1 Preheat oven to 240°C/220°C fan-forced. Oil two oven trays.
2 Boil, steam or microwave spinach until just wilted; drain on absorbent paper. Squeeze out excess liquid.
3 Heat oil in small frying pan, add onion and garlic; cook, stirring, until onion softens.
4 Combine spinach, onion mixture, rind, herbs and cheese in large bowl; mix well.
5 Place 1 sheet of pastry on each tray; divide spinach mixture between sheets, leaving a 3cm border. Using a metal spatula, fold pastry border roughly over edge of filling.
6 Bake pies about 20 minutes or until browned.

on the table in 35 minutes
serves 4 **per serving** 36.8g total fat (8.1g saturated fat); 2199kJ (526 cal); 33.4g carbohydrate; 14.5g protein; 3.5g fibre
tip for best results, use a pizza tray with holes in the base – this will make it possible to cook the pastry evenly.

Mushrooms with fetta on garlic croûtes

8 (500g) swiss brown mushrooms
½ cup (125ml) olive oil
200g cherry tomatoes, halved
8 slices crusty italian bread
1 clove garlic, peeled, halved
2 tablespoons shredded fresh basil
120g baby rocket leaves
80g fetta cheese, crumbled

1 Preheat oven 220°C/200°C fan-forced.
2 Brush mushrooms with ¼ cup (60ml) of the oil. Top mushrooms with tomato, cut-side up. Bake 10 minutes or until mushrooms are tender.
3 Brush bread with another 2 tablespoons of the oil and rub with garlic. Place in a single layer on an oven tray; bake about 5 minutes or until golden brown and crisp.
4 Pound (or blend in small food mill) basil and remaining 1 tablespoon oil in a mortar and pestle until combined.
5 Top croûtes with rocket, mushrooms and cheese; drizzle with basil mixture. Sprinkle with extra basil, if desired.

on the table in 20 minutes
serves 4 **per serving** 35.6g total fat (7.4g saturated fat); 2220kJ (531 cal); 35.2g carbohydrate; 15.0g protein; 6.6g fibre

Pumpkin and fetta pies

500g pumpkin, cut into 2cm pieces
3 eggs, beaten lightly
200g fetta cheese, cut into 2cm pieces
2 tablespoons finely grated parmesan cheese
2 tablespoons sour cream
1/3 cup (80g) drained char-grilled capsicum in oil, sliced thinly
2 tablespoons halved seeded kalamata olives
4 green onions, sliced thinly
1 sheet ready-rolled puff pastry, thawed
1 teaspoon finely shredded fresh basil

1 Preheat oven to 220°C/200°C fan-forced. Oil four 11cm pie dishes.
2 Boil, steam or microwave pumpkin until just tender; drain.
3 Combine egg, cheeses, sour cream, capsicum, olives and onion in large bowl. Add pumpkin; toss gently to combine.
4 Cut pastry sheet into four squares; press each square into pie dish, allowing pastry to hang over edge. Place dishes on oven tray; divide filling among dishes.
5 Bake pies, uncovered, about 15 minutes or until filling sets. Sprinkle with basil just before serving.

on the table in 30 minutes
serves 4 **per serving** 32.1g total fat (13.3g saturated fat); 1969kJ (471 cal); 24.9g carbohydrate; 20.4g protein; 2.1g fibre

Asparagus with tomato vinaigrette

600g asparagus, trimmed
2 medium ripe tomatoes (400g), peeled, seeded, chopped coarsely
¼ cup (40g) toasted pine nuts, chopped coarsely
⅓ cup loosely packed fresh baby basil leaves
dressing
⅓ cup (80ml) olive oil
1 tablespoon lemon juice
2 teaspoons dijon mustard

1 Boil, steam or microwave asparagus until just tender; drain.
2 Make dressing.
3 Combine dressing and tomato in medium bowl; stir well. Spoon over asparagus. Sprinkle with pine nuts and basil leaves.
dressing place ingredients in screw-top jar; shake well.

on the table in 15 minutes
serves 6 **per serving** 16.9g total fat (2.0g saturated fat); 727kJ (174 cal); 1.9g carbohydrate; 2.9g protein; 1.8g fibre

Mixed mushrooms in garlic butter

¼ cup (60ml) olive oil
1 large brown onion (200g), sliced thinly
2 cloves garlic, crushed
400g cap mushrooms, quartered
400g swiss brown mushrooms
400g button mushrooms
2 teaspoons garlic salt
50g butter, chopped coarsely
8 slices crusty italian bread

1 Preheat oven to 220°C/200°C fan-forced.
2 Heat 2 tablespoons of the oil in wok; stir-fry onion, garlic and mushrooms, until tender.
3 Add garlic salt and butter; stir-fry until butter melts.
4 Brush bread with remaining oil. Place in a single layer on an oven tray; bake about 5 minutes or until browned and crisp.
5 Serve mushroom mixture on toast, sprinkled with baby basil leaves, if desired.

on the table in 35 minutes
serves 4 **per serving** 26.7g total fat (9.0g saturated fat); 2023kJ (484 cal); 38.8g carbohydrate; 17.5g protein; 10.4g fibre

Bruschetta caprese

1 long loaf turkish bread
50g baby rocket leaves
250g cherry tomatoes, sliced thickly
100g baby bocconcini cheese, sliced thickly
2 tablespoons finely shredded fresh basil
2 tablespoons olive oil

1 Halve bread; reserve one half for another use. Cut remaining half crossways into four even-width pieces. Split each piece horizontally; toast both sides.
2 Top bread with equal amounts of rocket, tomato, cheese and basil; drizzle with oil.

on the table in 15 minutes
serves 4 **per serving** 16.6g total fat (4.3g saturated fat); 1743kJ (417 cal); 49.7g carbohydrate; 14.5g protein; 4.0g fibre

Corn and zucchini fritters with salsa

50g butter, melted
½ cup (125ml) milk
¾ cup (110g) plain flour
2 eggs, beaten lightly
210g can creamed corn
2 medium zucchini (240g), grated coarsely
vegetable oil, for shallow-frying
salsa
3 medium egg tomatoes (225g), chopped coarsely
2 medium avocados (500g), chopped coarsely
1 small red onion (100g), chopped coarsely
2 tablespoons lime juice
2 tablespoons finely chopped fresh coriander

1 Combine butter, milk, flour and egg in medium bowl; whisk until smooth. Add corn and zucchini; mix well.
2 Heat oil in large frying pan; cook heaped tablespoons of batter, about 2 minutes each side or until browned both sides and cooked through. Drain on absorbent paper.
3 Make salsa.
4 Serve fritters with salsa.
salsa combine ingredients in small bowl.

on the table in 20 minutes
serves 4 **per serving** 57.4g total fat (15.6g saturated fat); 2955kJ (707 cal); 34.1g carbohydrate; 11.9g protein; 6.2g fibre
tip keep cooked fritters warm in oven until serving time.

Tapenade and tomato pastries

2 sheets ready-rolled puff pastry
½ cup (60g) seeded black olives
2 teaspoons capers, rinsed, drained
2 teaspoons fresh lemon thyme leaves
2 teaspoons finely chopped fresh flat-leaf parsley
2 teaspoons olive oil
2 medium tomatoes (380g), sliced thinly
30g fetta cheese, crumbled
1 tablespoon fresh oregano leaves

1 Preheat oven to 200°C/180°C fan-forced. Line oven tray with baking paper.
2 Cut six 8.5cm rounds from each pastry sheet. Place on tray; using fork, score rounds five times, cover with baking paper, place another oven tray on top of pastry rounds. Bake, covered with tray, about 10 minutes or until browned.
3 Blend or process olives, capers, thyme, parsley and oil until tapenade is just combined.
4 Divide tomato among pastry bases; top each with 1 rounded teaspoon of the tapenade. Sprinkle with cheese and oregano.

on the table in 20 minutes
serves 4 **per serving** 23.2g total fat (2.9g saturated fat); 1601kJ (383 cal); 35.3g carbohydrate; 7.1g protein; 2.5g fibre
tip placing an oven tray on top of the pastry rounds while baking stops the pastry from puffing.

Pear, walnut and fetta salad with walnut oil dressing

We used william pears in this recipe, but you can use any variety you prefer.

3 medium pears (700g)
2 tablespoons coarsely chopped toasted walnuts
1 butter lettuce, trimmed, torn
½ cup (25g) snow pea sprouts
100g fetta cheese, crumbled
walnut oil dressing
1 tablespoon walnut oil
2 teaspoons wholegrain mustard
2 tablespoons white wine vinegar
1 clove garlic, crushed
1 tablespoon finely chopped fresh chives

1 Core pears; slice pears into thin wedges.

2 Make walnut oil dressing.

3 Place pears in large bowl with remaining ingredients and dressing; toss gently to combine.

walnut oil dressing place ingredients in screw-top jar; shake well.

on the table in 15 minutes
serves 4 **per serving** 13.9g total fat (4.4g saturated fat); 1028kJ (246 cal); 21.9g carbohydrate; 6.7g protein; 5.2g fibre

59

Corn fritters with rocket and avocado salad

You will need 2 large fresh corn cobs for this recipe.

1 cup (150g) self-raising flour
½ teaspoon bicarbonate of soda
1 cup (250ml) milk
2 eggs
2 cups (330g) fresh corn kernels
4 green onions, chopped finely
1 fresh small red thai chilli, chopped finely
tomato chilli sauce
425g can crushed tomatoes
1 tablespoon brown sugar
⅓ cup (80ml) sweet chilli sauce
2 tablespoons malt vinegar
rocket and avocado salad
100g baby rocket leaves
1 medium avocado (250g), sliced thinly
1 medium red onion (170g), sliced thinly
¼ cup (60ml) balsamic vinegar
1 tablespoon olive oil

1 Make tomato chilli sauce.
2 Sift flour and soda into medium bowl. Make well in centre of flour mixture; gradually whisk in combined milk and eggs until batter is smooth. Stir corn, onion and chilli into batter.
3 Pour ¼-cup of the batter onto heated oiled flat plate; using spatula, spread batter into a round. Cook about 2 minutes each side or until fritter is browned lightly and cooked through, remove from flat plate; cover to keep warm. Repeat with remaining batter.
4 Make rocket and avocado salad.
5 Serve corn fritters with tomato chilli sauce and salad.
tomato chilli sauce combine ingredients in medium frying pan; bring to a boil. Reduce heat; simmer, uncovered, 10 minutes or until sauce thickens.
rocket and avocado salad place rocket, avocado, onion and combined vinegar and oil in large bowl; toss gently to combine.

on the table in 30 minutes
serves 4 **per serving** 21.9g total fat (5.5g saturated fat); 2136kJ (511 cal); 57.0g carbohydrate; 15.9g protein; 9.1g fibre

Mediterranean vegetables and haloumi bruschetta

1 small french breadstick
1 tablespoon olive oil
1 small eggplant (230g), sliced thinly
200g haloumi cheese, sliced thinly
2 tablespoons plain flour
2 medium egg tomatoes (150g), sliced thinly
2 tablespoons fresh baby basil leaves
1 tablespoon baby capers, rinsed, drained

1 Preheat oven to 220°C/200°C fan-forced.
2 Cut bread, on an angle, into eight slices; brush both sides with half of the oil, place on oven tray. Bake about 5 minutes or until browned and crisp.
3 Cook eggplant on heated oiled grill plate (or grill or barbecue) until just tender.
4 Coat cheese in flour; cook on heated oiled grill plate (or grill or barbecue) until browned lightly.
5 Divide eggplant, cheese, tomato, basil and capers evenly among bruschetta. Drizzle with remaining oil.

on the table in 25 minutes
serves 4 **per serving** 14.6g total fat (6.3g saturated fat); 1225kJ (293 cal); 24.0g carbohydrate; 15.1g protein; 3.2g fibre

Sour cream and chive potato pancakes

It is important to squeeze as much excess moisture as possible from the potato so that the pancakes hold their shape while cooking.

900g potatoes, peeled
1 medium brown onion (150g), chopped finely
¼ cup finely chopped fresh chives
2 eggs, separated
2 tablespoons plain flour
½ cup (120g) sour cream
⅔ cup (160ml) vegetable oil
80g butter

1 Grate potatoes coarsely; squeeze excess moisture from potato with hands. Combine potato in large bowl with onion, chives, egg yolks, flour and sour cream.
2 Beat egg whites in small bowl with electric mixer until firm peaks form; gently fold into potato mixture.
3 Heat 2 tablespoons of the oil with 20g of the butter in large frying pan; cook heaped tablespoons of the potato mixture until browned both sides. Drain on absorbent paper; cover to keep warm. Repeat with the same amounts of remaining oil, butter and potato mixture.

on the table in 35 minutes
makes 20 **per pancake** 13.6g total fat (4.8g saturated fat); 660kJ (158 cal); 6.8g carbohydrate; 2.0g protein; 0.8g fibre

Vine-ripened tomatoes and goat cheese in walnut dressing

8 medium vine-ripened tomatoes (1.5kg), sliced thickly
150g goat cheese, sliced thickly
¼ cup (25g) walnuts, toasted, chopped coarsely
¼ cup (60ml) olive oil
1 clove garlic, crushed
1½ tablespoons raspberry vinegar
2 teaspoons dijon mustard
2 teaspoons coarsely chopped fresh thyme
2 teaspoons white sugar

1 Place one slice of tomato on each serving plate; top with a slice
of cheese.
2 Repeat layering, sprinkling nuts and combined remaining ingredients
between layers.

on the table in 15 minutes
serves 6 **per serving** 16.2g total fat (4.1g saturated fat); 857kJ (205 cal);
6.6g carbohydrate; 6.5g protein; 3.4g fibre
tips hazelnuts can be substituted for walnuts in this recipe, and,
if you have hazelnut or walnut oil on hand, use one of these, rather
than the olive oil.

Pear and fennel salad with honey mustard dressing

We used red sensation pears for this recipe.

100g baby spinach leaves
1 red oak leaf lettuce
2 baby fennel bulbs (320g), halved, sliced thinly
2 medium pears (375g), sliced thinly
¾ cup (60g) shaved parmesan cheese
honey mustard dressing
⅓ cup (80ml) olive oil
1 tablespoon sherry vinegar
1 teaspoon honey dijon mustard

1 Make honey mustard dressing.
2 Place spinach, lettuce, fennel, pears and cheese in large bowl with enough of the dressing to lightly coat leaves; toss gently to combine.
honey mustard dressing place ingredients in screw-top jar; shake well.

on the table in 15 minutes
serves 4 **per serving** 23.7 total fat (5.7g saturated fat); 1313kJ (314 cal); 14.4g carbohydrate; 8.7g protein; 6.7g fibre

Asparagus and pink grapefruit salad

It is important to buy young fresh asparagus for this salad, as it is served raw.

200g thin asparagus, trimmed
1 baby cos lettuce
1 medium avocado (250g), sliced thinly
2 pink grapefruit (800g), peeled, segmented
tarragon honey dressing
2 tablespoons olive oil
2 tablespoons tarragon vinegar
2 teaspoons honey
2 clove garlic, crushed

1 Cut asparagus spears in half crossways, then cut the tips into halves and the base into quarters lengthways.
2 Make tarragon honey dressing.
3 Arrange lettuce, avocado, grapefruit and asparagus on serving plates. Just before serving, drizzle with dressing.
tarragon honey dressing place ingredients in screw-top jar; shake well.

on the table in 20 minutes
serves 4 **per serving** 19.5g total fat (3.4g saturated fat); 1003kJ (240 cal); 10.8g carbohydrate; 3.6g protein; 3.1g fibre

Vegetable pesto pastries

2 sheets ready-rolled puff pastry, thawed
½ cup (125ml) sun-dried tomato pesto
280g jar antipasto char-grilled vegetables
6 medium egg tomatoes (450g), sliced lengthways
150g fetta cheese, crumbled

1 Preheat oven to 240°C/220°C fan-forced. Oil two oven trays.
2 Cut pastry sheets in half; place pieces on trays. Fold pastry edges in to make 1cm border. Spread pesto over centre of pastry.
3 Drain vegetables; pat dry with absorbent paper. Cut vegetables into strips. Arrange tomato and vegetables over centre of each piece of pastry; sprinkle with cheese.
4 Bake 10 minutes. Swap shelf position of trays; bake further 10 minutes or until pastry is puffed and browned.
5 Serve topped with fresh basil leaves, if desired.

on the table in 35 minutes
serves 4 **per serving** 44.9g total fat (10.2g saturated fat); 2571kJ (615 cal); 35.6g carbohydrate; 16.3g protein; 3.2g fibre

Poached eggs, pancetta and asparagus

4 slices pancetta
400g asparagus, trimmed
4 eggs
30g butter, melted
¼ cup (20g) parmesan cheese flakes

1 Cook pancetta under hot grill until crisp.
2 Boil, steam or microwave asparagus until just tender; drain.
3 Half-fill a large shallow frying pan with water; bring to a boil. Break eggs into cup, one at a time, then slide into pan. When all eggs are in pan, allow water to return to a boil. Cover pan, turn off heat; stand about 4 minutes or until a light film of egg white sets over yolks. Remove eggs, one at a time, using slotted spoon, and place on absorbent paper-lined saucer to blot up poaching liquid.
4 Divide asparagus among serving plates. Top with poached eggs and crumbled pancetta. Drizzle with butter and top with cheese. Sprinkle with freshly ground pepper, if desired.

on the table in 20 minutes
serves 4 **per serving** 15.1g total fat (7.5g saturated fat); 811kJ (194 cal); 1.2g carbohydrate; 13.2g protein; 1.0g fibre

soups

Cauliflower soup with cheese and bacon toasts

1 tablespoon olive oil
1 medium brown onion (150g), chopped coarsely
2 cloves garlic, crushed
1 large potato (300g), chopped finely
1kg cauliflower, trimmed, chopped
3 cups (750ml) chicken stock
3 cups (750ml) water
2 tablespoons coarsely chopped fresh chives
cheese and bacon toasts
3 thin bacon rashers, quartered
1 loaf thin crusty Italian bread
1 tablespoon wholegrain mustard
120g thinly sliced cheddar cheese

1 Heat olive oil in large saucepan; cook onion and garlic, stirring, until soft but not coloured.
2 Add potato, cauliflower, stock and water, bring to a boil; simmer, covered, until vegetables are very soft.
3 Blend or process cauliflower mixture, in batches, until smooth; return to same cleaned pan, stir until hot.
4 Make cheese and bacon toasts.
5 Serve soup with toasts, and sprinkled with chives.
cheese and bacon toasts place bacon on foil-lined oven tray; grill until browned and crisp. Slice bread diagonally into 12 thin slices; grill until browned lightly. Spread bread slices with mustard, top with cheese; grill until cheese melts, then top with bacon. Sprinkle with freshly ground black pepper, if desired.

on the table in 35 minutes
serves 6 **per serving** 13.6g total fat (5.6g saturated fat); 1513kJ (362 cal); 37.2g carbohydrate; 19.6g protein; 5.8g fibre
tip the smoothest consistency for this soup can be achieved by using a blender, stab mixer or mouli.

Pumpkin soup

40g butter
1 large brown onion (200g), chopped coarsely
3 bacon rashers (210g), chopped coarsely
1.5kg pumpkin, chopped coarsely
2 large potatoes (600g), chopped coarsely
1.5 litres (6 cups) chicken stock

1 Melt butter in large saucepan; cook onion and bacon, stirring, until onion softens.
2 Stir in pumpkin and potato.
3 Stir in stock, bring to a boil; simmer, uncovered, about 20 minutes or until pumpkin is soft.
4 Blend or process soup, in batches, until smooth; return to same cleaned pan, stir until hot.

on the table in 35 minutes
serves 6 **per serving** 8.4g total fat (5.1g saturated fat); 1066kJ (255 cal); 28.7g carbohydrate; 13.7g protein; 4.3g fibre
tip the smoothest consistency for this soup can be achieved by using a blender, stab mixer or mouli.

Hearty winter vegetable soup with couscous

Couscous, a fine-grained cereal product made from semolina, thickens this soup to a hearty consistency.

1 tablespoon olive oil
2 medium brown onions (300g), chopped coarsely
3 trimmed celery stalks (300g), chopped coarsely
1 clove garlic, crushed
1 teaspoon sweet paprika
3 medium potatoes (600g), chopped coarsely
2 large parsnips (700g), chopped coarsely
2 large carrots (360g), chopped coarsely
1½ cups (375ml) chicken stock
1.25 litres (5 cups) water
½ cup (100g) couscous
2 tablespoons coarsely chopped fresh flat-leaf parsley

1 Heat oil in large saucepan; cook onion, celery, garlic and paprika, stirring, until onion is soft.
2 Add potato, parsnip, carrot, stock and the water; bring to a boil. Reduce heat; simmer, covered, about 15 minutes or until vegetables are tender.
3 Stir in couscous and parsley; cook, uncovered, 2 minutes or until couscous is tender.

on the table in 30 minutes
serves 4 **per serving** 5.8g total fat (0.9g saturated fat); 1584kJ (379 cal); 63.0g carbohydrate; 12.5g protein; 10.9g fibre
tip couscous should be added just before serving as it will soak up the liquid.

Hot and sour soup

Straw mushrooms are a cultivated Chinese variety with an earthy flavour; they are usually sold canned in brine. Canned champignons or fresh baby button mushrooms can be substituted.

2cm piece fresh galangal (10g), chopped coarsely
10cm stick (20g) fresh lemon grass, chopped coarsely
2 green onions, chopped coarsely
3 fresh kaffir lime leaves
1 clove garlic, quartered
2 teaspoons peanut oil
1½ cups (375ml) vegetable stock
1.125 litres (4½ cups) water
2cm piece fresh ginger (10g), sliced thinly
2 fresh small red thai chillies, sliced thinly
425g canned straw mushrooms, drained, rinsed
2 teaspoons white sugar
⅓ cup (80ml) lime juice
2 teaspoons soy sauce
2 tablespoons finely chopped fresh coriander

1 Blend or process galangal, lemon grass, onion, lime leaves and garlic until chopped finely.
2 Heat oil in large saucepan; cook galangal mixture, stirring, until fragrant.
3 Add stock and the water; bring to a boil. Reduce heat; simmer, covered, 10 minutes. Strain stock mixture into large bowl; discard solids. Return stock mixture to same pan.
4 Return stock mixture to heat. Add ginger, chilli, mushrooms, sugar, juice and sauce; cook, uncovered, until hot. Just before serving, stir coriander through soup.

on the table in 25 minutes
serves 4 **per serving** 3.0g total fat (0.6g saturated fat); 284kJ (68 cal); 4.7g carbohydrate; 4.0g protein; 2.2g fibre

Kumara, chilli and coriander soup

100g fresh coriander, roots attached
1 tablespoon vegetable oil
1 large brown onion (200g), chopped coarsely
2 cloves garlic, crushed
1½ teaspoons sambal oelek
3 medium kumara (1.2kg), chopped coarsely
1 litre (4 cups) water
2 cups (500ml) chicken stock
⅔ cup (160ml) coconut milk

1 Wash coriander under cold running water, removing any dirt clinging to the roots; dry thoroughly. Finely chop enough of the coriander root to make 2 teaspoons (remaining root can be chopped, wrapped in plastic and frozen for future use); coarsely chop enough coriander leaves to make a loosely packed ¼ cup (freeze remainder of the leaves in the same way you do the roots).
2 Heat oil in large saucepan; cook coriander root, onion, garlic and sambal oelek, stirring, until onion softens.
3 Add kumara; cook, stirring, 5 minutes. Add the water and stock; bring to a boil. Reduce heat; simmer, uncovered, about 15 minutes or until kumara softens.
4 Blend or process soup, in batches, until smooth; return to same cleaned pan. Simmer, uncovered, over medium heat until thickened slightly; stir in coconut milk. Divide soup among serving bowls; sprinkle with reserved coriander leaves.

on the table in 30 minutes
serves 4 **per serving** 13.8g total fat (8.1g saturated fat); 1388kJ (332 cal); 41.7g carbohydrate; 7.9g protein; 6.4g fibre
tip the smoothest consistency for this soup can be achieved by using a blender, stab mixer or mouli.

Corn and bacon chowder

40g butter
1 medium brown onion (150g), chopped finely
1 clove garlic, crushed
2 bacon rashers (140g), chopped coarsely
¼ cup (35g) plain flour
2 medium potatoes (400g), chopped coarsely
2 cups (500ml) chicken stock
1 litre (4 cups) milk
2 cups (320g) frozen corn kernels
½ cup (125ml) cream
2 tablespoons finely chopped fresh chives

1 Heat butter in large saucepan; cook onion, garlic and bacon, stirring, until onion softens.
2 Stir in flour; cook, stirring, 1 minute. Stir in potato, stock and half of the milk; simmer, covered, about 15 minutes or until potato is soft.
3 Add corn, remaining milk and cream; cook, stirring, until hot. Stir in chives.

on the table in 35 minutes
serves 4 **per serving** 34.2g total fat (21.5g saturated fat); 2475kJ (592 cal); 47.5g carbohydrate; 21.6g protein; 6.0g fibre

Lentil and caramelised onion soup

2 cups (400g) red lentils
½ cup (100g) brown rice
1 litre (4 cups) vegetable stock
1 litre (4 cups) water
1 tablespoon ground cumin
40g butter
3 medium brown onions (450g), sliced thinly
2 tablespoons white sugar
1 tablespoon balsamic vinegar
pinch cayenne pepper
⅓ cup finely chopped fresh coriander
⅓ cup finely chopped fresh flat-leaf parsley
1 cup (250ml) vegetable stock, extra

1 Rinse lentils and rice under cold water; drain.
2 Combine stock and the water in large saucepan; bring to a boil. Add lentils, rice and cumin; return to a boil. Reduce heat; simmer, uncovered, stirring occasionally, 15 minutes or until lentils and rice are just tender.
3 Melt butter in large frying pan; cook onion, stirring, until onion softens. Add sugar and vinegar; cook, stirring, until onion caramelises.
4 Stir pepper, coriander, parsley, caramelised onion and extra stock into lentil mixture; cook, stirring, until heated through.

on the table in 35 minutes
serves 4 **per serving** 12.2g total fat (6.5g saturated fat); 2316kJ (554 cal); 74.2g carbohydrate; 31.5g protein; 16.3g fibre

Minestrone

2 teaspoons olive oil
1 small brown onion (80g), chopped coarsely
2 cloves garlic, crushed
2 trimmed celery stalks (200g), chopped coarsely
1 small carrot (70g), chopped coarsely
1 small zucchini (90g) chopped coarsely
810g can crushed tomatoes
1 medium potato (200g), chopped coarsely
2½ cups (625ml) chicken stock
1½ cups (375ml) water
1 cup (180g) macaroni pasta
½ cup (100g) canned red kidney beans, rinsed, drained
1 cup (80g) finely shredded wombok
1 cup (40g) coarsely shredded spinach leaves
½ cup shredded fresh basil
½ cup (40g) coarsely grated parmesan cheese

1 Heat oil in large saucepan; cook onion and garlic, stirring occasionally, until onion softens.
2 Add celery, carrot and zucchini; cook, stirring, 5 minutes. Stir in undrained tomatoes, potato, stock and the water; bring to a boil. Add pasta; simmer, uncovered, 15 minutes or until potato and pasta are just tender.
3 Stir beans through soup until hot. Just before serving, stir wombok, spinach and basil into minestrone; serve sprinkled with cheese.

on the table in 30 minutes
serves 4 **per serving** 7.5g total fat (2.8g saturated fat); 1509kJ (361 cal); 51.4g carbohydrate; 16.5g protein; 9.0g fibre

Zucchini cream soup

30g butter
1 large brown onion (200g), chopped finely
2 cloves garlic, crushed
8 large zucchini (1.2kg), chopped coarsely
2 tablespoons plain flour
1½ cups (375ml) chicken stock
1 cup (250ml) water
½ cup (125ml) cream

1 Melt butter in large saucepan; cook onion and garlic, stirring, until onion softens. Stir in zucchini and flour; cook, stirring, 2 minutes.
2 Stir in stock and the water, bring to a boil; simmer, uncovered, about 15 minutes or until zucchini is tender.
3 Blend or process soup, in batches, until smooth; return to same cleaned pan. Add cream; stir over medium heat until hot.
4 Serve soup topped with chervil, if desired.

on the table in 35 minutes
serves 4 **per serving** 21.2g total fat (13.2g saturated fat); 1162kJ (278 cal); 13.3g carbohydrate; 6.7g protein; 5.9g fibre
tip the smoothest consistency for this soup can be achieved by using a blender, stab mixer or mouli.

Vegetable and red lentil soup

2 tablespoons mild curry paste
400g can tomatoes
3 cups (750ml) chicken stock
1 large carrot (180g), chopped finely
2 trimmed celery stalks (200g), chopped finely
1 medium potato (200g), chopped finely
1 large zucchini (150g), chopped finely
¾ cup (150g) red lentils
½ cup (60g) frozen peas
⅓ cup (80ml) light coconut milk
2 tablespoons finely chopped fresh coriander

1 Cook curry paste in heated large saucepan, stirring, about 1 minute or until fragrant. Add undrained crushed tomatoes, stock, carrot, celery, potato and zucchini; bring to a boil. Reduce heat; simmer, covered, 5 minutes.
2 Add lentils to soup mixture; return to a boil. Reduce heat; simmer, uncovered, about 10 minutes or until lentils are just tender. Add peas; return to a boil. Reduce heat; simmer, uncovered, until peas are just tender.
3 Remove soup from heat; stir in remaining ingredients.

on the table in 30 minutes
serves 6 **per serving** 5.3g total fat (2.0g saturated fat); 782kJ (187 cal); 20.9g carbohydrate; 10.6g protein; 7.7g fibre
tip a hotter curry paste or some finely chopped chilli can be added to boost the flavour.

Pea and potato soup

30g butter
1 small leek (200g), sliced thinly
2 trimmed celery stalks (200g), chopped coarsely
3 large potatoes (900g), chopped coarsely
3 cups (750ml) chicken stock
2 cups (500ml) water
2 cups (250g) frozen peas
⅓ cup (80ml) cream
1 tablespoon fresh thyme leaves

1 Melt butter in large saucepan; cook leek and celery, stirring, until soft.
2 Add potato, stock and the water. Cover; bring to a boil. Reduce heat; simmer, stirring occasionally, about 15 minutes or until potato softens.
3 Add peas; cook, uncovered, about 5 minutes or until peas are tender.
4 Blend or process soup, in batches, until smooth; return to same cleaned pan. Add cream and thyme; stir until hot.

on the table in 30 minutes
serves 4 **per serving** 16.2g total fat (10.1g saturated fat); 1450kJ (347 cal); 34.4g carbohydrate; 11.9g protein; 8.5g fibre
tip the smoothest consistency for this soup will be achieved by using a blender, stab mixer or mouli.

Lentil and spinach soup

2 tablespoons peanut oil
2 large brown onions (400g), chopped finely
2 cloves garlic, crushed
2 teaspoons ground cumin
1 teaspoon ground turmeric
1 teaspoon ground coriander
3 cups (600g) red lentils
1.25 litres (5 cups) chicken stock
1 litre (4 cups) water
500g spinach, trimmed, chopped finely

1 Heat oil in large saucepan; cook onion and garlic, stirring, until onion is soft. Add spices; cook, stirring, until fragrant.
2 Add lentils; stir to combine with spice mixture. Add stock and the water; bring to a boil. Simmer soup, uncovered, about 20 minutes or until lentils are tender.
3 Blend or process soup, in batches, until smooth; return soup to same cleaned pan. Add spinach; stir over heat until hot.

on the table in 35 minutes
serves 8 **per serving** 6.9g total fat (1.4g saturated fat); 1225kJ (293 cal); 32.5g carbohydrate; 21.4g protein; 11.9g fibre
tip the smoothest consistency for this soup can be achieved by using a blender, stab mixer or mouli.

Asian mushroom broth

Other varieties of mushrooms, such as button or shimeji, can also be used in this recipe.

cooking-oil spray
4 green onions, chopped finely
1 trimmed celery stalk (100g), chopped finely
1.5 litres (6 cups) chicken stock
1½ cups (375ml) water
¼ cup (60ml) light soy sauce
100g shiitake mushrooms, sliced thinly
100g enoki mushrooms, trimmed
150g oyster mushrooms, sliced thinly
150g swiss brown mushrooms, sliced thinly
½ teaspoon five-spice powder
2 tablespoons finely chopped fresh garlic chives

1 Spray heated large saucepan with cooking-oil spray; cook onion and celery, stirring, until vegetables soften.
2 Add stock, the water and sauce; bring to a boil. Add mushrooms and five-spice; return to a boil. Reduce heat; simmer 2 minutes or until mushrooms soften.
3 Just before serving, sprinkle with chives.

on the table in 20 minutes
serves 4 **per serving** 1.9g total fat (0.8g saturated fat); 364kJ (87 cal); 5.7g carbohydrate; 9.7g protein; 4.5g fibre

Sweet potato soup

25g butter
1 medium brown onion (150g), chopped coarsely
2 cloves garlic, quartered
2 bacon rashers (140g), chopped coarsely
½ cup (125ml) dry white wine
2 large potatoes (600g), chopped coarsely
3 small kumara (750g), chopped coarsely
3 cups (750ml) chicken stock
2 cups (500ml) water
¼ cup (60ml) cream
2 teaspoons finely chopped fresh rosemary

1 Melt butter in large saucepan; cook onion, garlic and bacon, stirring, until onion softens.
2 Add wine, potato and kumara; bring to a boil. Reduce heat; simmer, stirring, 2 minutes.
3 Add stock and the water; return soup to a boil. Reduce heat; simmer, covered, 15 minutes or until vegetables soften.
4 Blend or process soup mixture, in batches, until smooth; return to same cleaned pan. Add cream and rosemary; stir until hot. Serve sprinkled with more fresh rosemary, if desired.

on the table in 35 minutes
serves 4 **per serving** 13.8g total fat (8.4g saturated fat); 1618kJ (387 cal); 44.5g carbohydrate; 13.3g protein; 5.8g fibre
tip the smoothest consistency for this soup can be achieved by using a blender, stab mixer or mouli.

Spring vegetable soup

1 tablespoon olive oil
1 small brown onion (80g), chopped finely
1 clove garlic, crushed
350g baby carrots, sliced thickly
3 cups (750ml) chicken stock
2 cups (500ml) water
¼ cup (55g) farfalline, risoni or any small soup pasta
200g asparagus, trimmed, sliced thickly
1 cup (125g) frozen peas
⅓ cup (25g) grated parmesan cheese
1 tablespoon finely chopped fresh chives

1 Heat oil in large saucepan; cook onion and garlic, stirring, until onion softens. Add carrot; cook, stirring, 2 minutes.
2 Add stock and the water; bring to a boil. Stir in pasta; simmer, uncovered, about 8 minutes or until tender. Return to a boil, add asparagus and peas; simmer, uncovered, until tender.
3 Serve sprinkled with cheese and chives.

on the table in 30 minutes
serves 4 **per serving** 7.8g total fat (2.3g saturated fat); 798kJ (191 cal); 18.2g carbohydrate; 9.6g protein; 5.4g fibre
tip if the soup thickens on standing, add a little more water or stock.

Cream of roasted garlic and potato soup

2 medium garlic bulbs (140g), unpeeled
2 tablespoons olive oil
2 medium brown onions (300g), chopped coarsely
1 tablespoon fresh thyme leaves
5 medium potatoes (1kg), chopped coarsely
1.25 litres (5 cups) chicken stock
¾ cup (180ml) cream

1 Preheat oven to 180°C/160°C fan-forced.
2 Separate garlic bulbs into cloves; place unpeeled cloves, in single layer, on oven tray. Drizzle with half of the oil. Roast, uncovered, 15 minutes or until garlic is soft. When cool enough to handle, squeeze garlic into small bowl; discard skins.
3 Heat remaining oil in large saucepan; cook onion and thyme, stirring, until onion softens. Add potato and stock; bring to a boil. Reduce heat; simmer, uncovered, about 15 minutes or until potato is just tender. Stir in garlic; simmer, uncovered, 5 minutes.
4 Blend or process soup, in batches, until smooth; return to same cleaned pan. Stir until hot then add cream. Divide soup among serving bowls; sprinkle with extra thyme, if desired.

on the table in 35 minutes
serves 4 **per serving** 27.9g total fat (13g saturated fat); 1864kJ (446 cal); 36.8g carbohydrate; 12g protein; 8.5g fibre
tip the smoothest consistency for this soup can be achieved by using a blender, stab mixer or mouli.

109

Tomato, capsicum and bean soup

1 tablespoon olive oil
2 medium brown onions (300g), chopped coarsely
1 large red capsicum (350g), chopped coarsely
1 medium fresh red chilli, chopped finely
810g can crushed tomatoes
1 litre (4 cups) chicken stock
2 x 300g cans butter beans, rinsed, drained

1 Heat oil in large saucepan; cook onion, capsicum and chilli, stirring, until vegetables are very soft.
2 Add undrained tomatoes and stock; bring to a boil. Reduce heat; simmer, covered, about 15 minutes or until thickened slightly.
3 Blend or process soup, in batches, until smooth; return to same cleaned pan. Add beans; stir until hot.
4 Serve soup with garlic bread, if desired.

on the table in 30 minutes
serves 6 **per serving** 4.3g total fat (0.8g saturated fat); 489kJ (117 cal); 11.7g carbohydrate; 6.0g protein; 4.2g fibre
tips cans labelled butter beans are, in fact, cannellini beans. In place of butter beans, try kidney beans, chickpeas or small pasta, if desired.

salads

Red cabbage, apple and caraway coleslaw

This salad can be served either warm or cold.

2 medium green apples (300g)
½ medium red cabbage (800g), shredded finely
2 tablespoons caraway seeds, toasted
2 teaspoons dijon mustard
½ cup (125ml) olive oil
2 tablespoons raspberry vinegar

1 Core unpeeled apples; cut into matchstick-size pieces.
2 Place apple in large bowl with cabbage and seeds; drizzle with combined remaining ingredients. Toss gently to combine.

on the table in 15 minutes
serves 8 **per serving** 14.6g total fat (2.0g saturated fat); 723kJ (173 cal); 6.4g carbohydrate; 2.3g protein; 4.5g fibre
tip if your supermarket doesn't stock raspberry vinegar, use any fruit-flavoured vinegar in this recipe.

White bean salad with coriander, mint and lemon grass

2 x 400g cans cannellini beans, rinsed, drained
150g baby spinach leaves
1 small red onion (100g), sliced thinly
2 fresh small red thai chillies, sliced thinly
dressing
1 clove garlic, crushed
1 tablespoon coarsely chopped fresh coriander
1 tablespoon coarsely chopped fresh mint
10cm stick (20g) fresh lemon grass, sliced thinly
1cm piece fresh ginger (5g), grated finely
2 tablespoons sesame oil
2 tablespoons soy sauce
2 tablespoons sweet chilli sauce
2 tablespoons lime juice
1 teaspoon honey

1 Combine beans in large bowl with spinach and onion.
2 Make dressing.
3 Just before serving, drizzle dressing over salad; toss gently to combine, then sprinkle with chilli.
dressing place ingredients in screw-top jar; shake well.

on the table in 15 minutes
serves 4 **per serving** 10.5g total fat (1.4g saturated fat); 995kJ (238 cal); 19.8g carbohydrate; 10.4g protein; 10.7g fibre

Crispy noodle cabbage salad

Crunchy or fried noodles are available round or flat – either can be used in this salad.

3 cups (240g) finely shredded white cabbage
3 cups (240g) finely shredded red cabbage
300g packet crunchy noodles
8 green onions, chopped finely
½ cup finely chopped fresh flat-leaf parsley
2 tablespoons sesame seeds, toasted
dressing
1 tablespoon sesame oil
1 tablespoon peanut oil
2 tablespoons white vinegar
2 tablespoons light soy sauce
½ cup (125ml) sweet chilli sauce

1 Place cabbages, noodles, onion, parsley and seeds in large bowl.
2 Make dressing.
3 Pour dressing over salad; toss gently to combine.
dressing place ingredients in screw-top jar; shake well.

on the table in 15 minutes
serves 4 **per serving** 20.2g total fat (4.8g saturated fat); 1400kJ (335 cal); 26.1g carbohydrate; 7.3g protein; 9.6g fibre
tips make this salad just before serving or the noodles will lose their crispness.

Watercress salad

We used corella pears for this recipe. You will need a bunch of watercress weighing about 350g in total to yield the leaves required for this salad.

3 small pears (375g), sliced thinly
1 teaspoon finely grated orange rind
½ cup (125ml) orange juice
300g snow peas, trimmed
100g watercress leaves
cheese balls
150g low-fat ricotta cheese
100g low-fat fetta cheese
¼ cup (30g) finely grated cheddar cheese
1 tablespoon finely chopped fresh flat-leaf parsley
1 tablespoon finely chopped fresh chives
2 teaspoons finely chopped fresh thyme
1 teaspoon curry powder
1 teaspoon sweet paprika

1 Combine pear, rind and juice in large bowl. Cover; refrigerate 15 minutes.
2 Boil, steam or microwave snow peas until just tender; drain. Rinse under cold water; drain.
3 Make cheese balls.
4 Gently toss pear mixture, snow peas and watercress in large bowl. Serve topped with cheese balls.
cheese balls combine cheeses, parsley, chives and thyme in small bowl. Roll level teaspoons of mixture into balls. Combine curry powder and paprika in small bowl; gently toss half of the cheese balls in curry mixture until coated.

on the table in 30 minutes
serves 6 **per serving** 6.5g total fat (4.0g saturated fat); 686kJ (164 cal); 14.7g carbohydrate; 10.4g protein; 3.6g fibre

Cabbage, fennel and carrot salad with orange-herb dressing

You will need to buy a quarter of a medium red cabbage and a medium wombok for this recipe.

4 trimmed celery stalks (400g)
2 medium carrots (240g)
2 small fennel bulbs (400g), trimmed, sliced thinly
4 trimmed red radishes (60g), sliced thinly
1½ cups (120g) finely shredded red cabbage
5 cups (400g) coarsely shredded wombok
1 cup loosely packed fresh basil leaves
1 cup loosely packed fresh mint leaves
¼ cup (40g) pepitas
orange-herb dressing
1 tablespoon finely chopped fresh flat-leaf parsley
4 green onions, chopped coarsely
½ teaspoon finely grated orange rind
⅓ cup (80ml) orange juice
2 tablespoons raspberry vinegar
2 cloves garlic, crushed
1 tablespoon peanut oil

1 Make orange-herb dressing.
2 Cut celery and carrot into 6cm lengths; using vegetable peeler, slice celery and carrot into ribbons.
3 Place ribbons in large bowl with fennel, radish, cabbage, wombok, herbs and dressing; toss gently to combine. Sprinkle with pepitas.
orange-herb dressing place ingredients in screw-top jar; shake well.

on the table in 20 minutes
serves 4 **per serving** 8.4g total fat (0.9g saturated fat); 761kJ (182 cal); 11.2g carbohydrate; 4.2g protein; 9.9g fibre

Rocket and avocado salad

100g wild rocket leaves
200g grape tomatoes, halved
1 large avocado (320g), chopped coarsely
1 small red onion (100g), sliced thinly
150g bocconcini cheese, torn
2 tablespoons toasted pine nuts
creamy dressing
2 tablespoons mayonnaise
1 tablespoon lemon juice
1 tablespoon water
4 anchovy fillets, chopped finely
1 clove garlic, crushed

1 Make creamy dressing.
2 Place rocket and remaining ingredients in large bowl with dressing;
toss gently to combine.
creamy dressing whisk ingredients in small bowl until smooth.

on the table in 20 minutes
serves 6 **per serving** 17.9g total fat (4.8g saturated fat); 865kJ (207 cal);
3.7g carbohydrate; 7.3g protein; 1.9g fibre

Creamy potato salad

2kg potatoes, washed
3 bacon rashers, chopped finely
1½ cups (450g) mayonnaise
1 teaspoon coarse salt
2 tablespoons olive oil
¼ cup (60ml) white wine vinegar
4 hard-boiled eggs
½ cup coarsely chopped fresh flat-leaf parsley

1 Boil, steam or microwave potatoes until tender, drain; cool. Slice potatoes thickly and place in large bowl.
2 Fry bacon, uncovered, in dry heated pan until browned and crisp; drain on absorbent paper.
3 Whisk mayonnaise, salt, oil and vinegar in medium bowl until smooth.
4 Cut eggs into eighths lengthways.
5 Close to serving, combine potatoes, bacon, dressing, eggs and parsley.

on the table in 35 minutes
serves 8 **per serving** 26.4g total fat (3.9g saturated fat); 1998kJ (478 cal); 43.9g carbohydrate; 12.9g protein; 5.5g fibre

Mushroom and chive salad

600g button mushrooms, sliced thinly
¼ cup coarsely chopped fresh chives
¼ cup coarsely chopped fresh flat-leaf parsley
dressing
1 teaspoon finely grated lemon rind
2 tablespoons lemon juice
⅓ cup (80ml) olive oil
½ teaspoon drained green peppercorns, chopped finely

1 Make dressing.
2 Place mushrooms and herbs in medium bowl with dressing;
toss gently to combine.
dressing place ingredients in screw-top jar; shake well.

on the table in 15 minutes
serves 8 **per serving** 9.3g total fat (1.3g saturated fat); 435kJ (104 cal);
1.3g carbohydrate; 2.8g protein; 2.0g fibre
tip salad can be made up to 2 hours ahead.

Teardrop tomato salad

Any type of pesto can be used in the dressing.

500g asparagus, trimmed, halved
250g cherry tomatoes, halved
500g yellow teardrop tomatoes, halved
100g rocket leaves
2 small avocados (400g), sliced thickly
⅓ cup finely shredded fresh basil
dressing
⅓ cup (80ml) olive oil
1 tablespoon white vinegar
1 tablespoon basil pesto
1 clove garlic, crushed

1 Boil, steam or microwave asparagus until just tender; drain. Rinse under cold water; drain.
2 Make dressing.
3 Place asparagus in large bowl with tomatoes, rocket, avocado, basil and dressing; toss gently to combine.
dressing place ingredients in screw-top jar; shake well.

on the table in 15 minutes
serves 4 **per serving** 36.5g total fat (6.4g saturated fat); 1609kJ (385 cal); 6.3g carbohydrate; 5.6g protein; 6.0g fibre
tip asparagus can be prepared in advance and refrigerated, covered, until just before assembling salad.

Potato and beetroot salad

3 large potatoes (750g)
1 small fresh beetroot (90g)
⅓ cup (40g) frozen peas
3 hard-boiled eggs, quartered
¾ cup (210g) yogurt
1 tablespoon coarsely chopped fresh dill
1 tablespoon coarsely chopped fresh flat-leaf parsley
2 large dill pickles, chopped coarsely
1 small red onion (100g), chopped finely

1 Boil, steam or microwave potatoes until just tender; drain. Cool; cut into 2cm cubes.
2 Boil, steam or microwave beetroot and peas, separately, until just tender; drain. Cool; chop beetroot coarsely.
3 Place potato and beetroot in medium bowl with peas and remaining ingredients; toss gently to combine.

on the table in 35 minutes
serves 4 **per serving** 6.3g total fat (2.4g saturated fat); 1028kJ (246 cal); 30.8g carbohydrate; 13.0g protein; 4.5g fibre
tips canned whole baby beets can be substituted for fresh beetroot, if preferred. Potatoes, beetroot and peas can be cooked in advance and refrigerated, covered. Combine salad just before serving or beetroot will "bleed" into egg and potato.

Warm potato and chorizo salad

16 chat potatoes (600g), halved
3 chorizo (350g), sliced thinly
2 tablespoons olive oil
½ cup (125ml) balsamic vinegar
2 teaspoons white sugar
1 small red onion (100g), sliced thinly
200g baby spinach leaves
250g cherry tomatoes, halved

1 Boil, steam or microwave potato about 10 minutes or until tender; drain.
2 Fry chorizo in a dry heated frying pan until crisp on both sides; remove from pan.
3 Add potato to same pan; cook, stirring gently, until browned. Remove from pan.
4 Remove pan from heat, add combined oil, vinegar and sugar to pan. Return to heat, boil, uncovered, for 2 minutes or until reduced slightly.
5 Place potato and chorizo in large bowl with onion, spinach and tomatoes; drizzle with vinegar mixture. Toss gently to combine.

on the table in 35 minutes
serves 4 **per serving** 35.7g total fat (10.8g saturated fat); 2232kJ (534 cal); 27.2g carbohydrate; 22.5g protein; 6.0g fibre

Beetroot, asparagus and fetta salad

340g asparagus, trimmed, halved
1 cup loosely packed fresh mint leaves, torn
450g can beetroot wedges, drained
200g fetta cheese, crumbled
½ cup (50g) walnut halves, toasted
lemon dressing
1 clove garlic, crushed
¼ cup (60ml) olive oil
1½ tablespoons lemon juice

1 Boil, steam or microwave asparagus until just tender; drain.
2 Make lemon dressing.
3 Place asparagus in large bowl with mint, beetroot, three-quarters of the cheese, nuts and dressing; toss gently to combine. Top with remaining cheese.
lemon dressing place ingredients in screw-top jar; shake well.

on the table in 15 minutes
serves 6 **per serving** 22.8g total fat (6.8g saturated fat); 1129kJ (270 cal); 6.2g carbohydrate; 9.1g protein; 3.1g fibre

Fattoush

6 pocket pitta bread (500g)
olive oil, for shallow-frying
3 medium tomatoes (450g), chopped coarsely
1 large green capsicum (350g), chopped coarsely
2 lebanese cucumbers (260g), seeded, sliced thinly
10 trimmed red radishes (150g), sliced thinly
4 spring onions, sliced thinly
1½ cups firmly packed fresh flat-leaf parsley leaves
½ cup coarsely chopped fresh mint
lemon garlic dressing
2 cloves garlic, crushed
¼ cup (60ml) olive oil
¼ cup (60ml) lemon juice

1 Halve pitta horizontally; cut into 2.5cm pieces. Heat oil in wok; shallow-fry pitta, in batches, until browned lightly and crisp. Drain on absorbent paper.
2 Make lemon garlic dressing.
3 Just before serving, place about three-quarters of the pitta in large bowl with dressing and remaining ingredients; toss gently to combine. Sprinkle remaining pitta over fattoush.
lemon garlic dressing place ingredients in screw-top jar; shake well.

on the table in 35 minutes
serves 4 **per serving** 30.5g total fat (4.2g saturated fat); 2692kJ (644 cal); 72.5g carbohydrate; 15.4g protein; 8.4g fibre
tips for a lower-fat alternative, spray pitta pieces with cooking-oil spray then bake, uncovered, at 220°C/200°C fan-forced until crisp; break into small pieces over salad.

Bacon, egg and endive salad with shallot mayonnaise

4 bacon rashers, sliced thinly
150g baby green beans, trimmed, halved
300g baby endive
½ x 170g packet baker chips or mini bagel crisps
4 medium-boiled eggs, quartered
shallot mayonnaise
1 egg
1 tablespoon chopped fresh dill
1 teaspoon dijon mustard
1 tablespoon lemon juice
½ cup (125ml) olive oil
1 french shallot, chopped finely

1 Pan-fry bacon until crisp. Boil, steam or microwave beans until tender; rinse, drain.
2 Make shallot mayonnaise.
3 Combine endive, bacon, beans and bagel crisps in large bowl. Top with egg and mayonnaise.
shallot mayonnaise fill small saucepan with cold water; add egg, bring to boil. Boil for 1 minute. Drain; rinse with cold water. Remove shell from top of egg. Process dill, mustard and juice until combined. Scoop out egg, add to processor. Slowly add oil with motor operating. Stir in shallot.

on the table in 35 minutes
serves 6 as an entree **per serving** 27.0g total fat (4.8g saturated fat); 1455kJ (348 cal); 11.6g carbohydrate; 14.2g protein; 1.8g fibre

Chinese potato salad

Purple shallots are often found under the name of thai, asian or even pink shallots. Used throughout South-East Asia, they are a member of the onion family but resemble garlic in that they grow in multiple-clove bulbs and are intensely flavoured. They can be eaten fresh in salads or deep-fried and served as a condiment.

1kg potatoes, quartered
8 green onions, sliced thinly
5 purple shallots, sliced thinly
½ cup loosely packed fresh coriander leaves
½ cup coarsely chopped fresh mint
2 fresh small red thai chillies, sliced thinly
sesame lime dressing
¼ cup (60ml) lime juice
1 egg yolk
1 teaspoon sesame oil
¾ cup (180ml) peanut oil
2 teaspoons mirin
2 tablespoons finely chopped fresh coriander

1 Boil, steam or microwave potato until just tender; drain.
2 Make sesame lime dressing.
3 Place warm potato in large bowl with remaining ingredients and dressing; toss gently to combine.
sesame lime dressing blend or process 1 tablespoon of the juice with egg yolk until slightly thickened. With motor operating, gradually add oils in a thin, steady stream; process until mixture thickens. Stir in remaining juice and remaining ingredients.

on the table in 35 minutes
serves 4 **per serving** 44.0g total fat (8.0g saturated fat); 2441kJ (584 cal); 35.7g carbohydrate; 8.1g protein; 6.5g fibre

Two-tomato salad

400g grape or cherry tomatoes
250g yellow teardrop tomatoes, halved
½ cup baby basil leaves
2 tablespoons balsamic vinegar

1 Combine all ingredients in medium serving bowl.

on the table in 5 minutes
serves 8 **per serving** 0.1g total fat (0.0g saturated fat); 59kJ (14 cal);
1.8g carbohydrate; 0.4g protein; 1.4g fibre

Mixed greens, cucumber and mint salad

Vietnamese mint, also known as cambodian mint and laksa leaf, is a pungent, narrow-leafed herb frequently used in many South-East Asian soups and salads.

4 lebanese cucumbers (520g)
2 medium butter lettuce, trimmed
2 medium radicchio (400g), trimmed
½ cup vietnamese mint leaves
1 red banana chilli, chopped finely
5cm stick (10g) fresh lemon grass, sliced thinly
½ cup (125ml) peanut oil
3 teaspoons sesame oil
1 tablespoon raw sugar
2 teaspoons finely grated lime rind
¼ cup (60ml) lime juice

1 Cut cucumbers diagonally into thin slices.
2 Place cucumber, lettuce leaves and mint in large bowl with combined remaining ingredients; toss gently to combine.

on the table in 15 minutes
serves 8 **per serving** 16.2g total fat (2.8g saturated fat); 727kJ (174 cal); 4.4g carbohydrate; 1.5g protein; 2.8g fibre
tips fresh mint can be substituted for vietnamese mint in this recipe.
Banana chilli is a sweet-flavoured chilli with a long, tapering shape.
If unavailable, replace with red capsicum.

Tomato and radish salad

250g yellow teardrop tomatoes
250g red grape tomatoes
5 medium egg tomatoes (375g), chopped coarsely
6 red radishes (210g), sliced thinly
1 medium red onion (170g), sliced thinly
100g pitted green olives, sliced
¼ cup small fresh basil leaves
2 tablespoons red wine vinegar
1 tablespoon olive oil

1 Place ingredients in large bowl; toss gently to combine.

on the table in 15 minutes
serves 10 **per serving** 3.5g total fat (0.5g saturated fat); 339kJ (81 cal); 8.9g carbohydrate; 1.8g protein; 3.0g fibre
tip this recipe can be prepared several hours ahead. Add basil, vinegar and oil close to serving.

Green salad with fennel and herbs

1 baby cos lettuce, shredded
200g baby rocket leaves
100g watercress
5 green onions, chopped
1 small fennel bulb (200g), sliced thinly
¼ cup coarsely chopped fresh dill
½ cup loosely packed fresh mint leaves
½ cup (80g) pine nuts, toasted
dressing
¼ cup (60ml) olive oil
¼ cup (60ml) red wine vinegar

1 Make dressing.
2 Place lettuce, rocket, watercress, green onions, fennel and herbs in large bowl with pine nuts and dressing; toss gently to combine.
dressing place ingredients in screw-top jar; shake well.

on the table in 15 minutes
serves 8 **per serving** 14.2g total fat (1.4g saturated fat); 640kJ (153 cal); 2.4g carbohydrate; 3.0g protein; 2.6g fibre

Avocado caprese salad

4 large vine-ripened tomatoes (480g)
250g cherry bocconcini cheese
1 large avocado (320g), halved
¼ cup loosely packed fresh basil leaves
2 tablespoons olive oil
1 tablespoon balsamic vinegar

1 Slice tomatoes, cheese and avocado thickly.
2 Place slices of tomato, cheese and avocado on serving platter; top with basil, drizzle with combined oil and vinegar. Sprinkle with freshly ground black pepper, if desired.

on the table in 10 minutes
serves 4 **per serving** 31.4g total fat (10.3g saturated fat); 1455kJ (348 cal); 2.5g carbohydrate; 13.1g protein; 2.4g fibre
tip we used vine-ripened truss tomatoes because it takes a simple recipe like this for their brilliant colour, robust flavour and crisp, tangy flesh to stand out at their magnificent best. Always go for vine-ripened tomatoes when serving them raw – use less costly ones for cooking.

Asparagus and broad bean salad

300g asparagus, trimmed, halved lengthways
500g frozen broad beans
1 green oak leaf lettuce
1 baby cos lettuce
1 baby endive
1 cup (170g) pecans, toasted
dressing
⅓ cup (80ml) lemon juice
⅔ cup (160ml) olive oil
1 teaspoon caster sugar
2 tablespoons finely chopped fresh flat-leaf parsley
2 tablespoons finely chopped fresh chives

1 Boil, steam or microwave asparagus until just tender; drain.
2 Pour boiling water over broad beans; drain well. Peel.
3 Make dressing.
4 On a large serving platter or bowl, arrange lettuce, endive, asparagus and broad beans. Drizzle with dressing; top with pecans.
dressing place ingredients in screw-top jar; shake well.

on the table in 30 minutes
serves 10 **per serving** 27.2g total fat (2.8g saturated fat); 1300kJ (311 cal); 6.9g carbohydrate; 6.3g protein; 8.0g fibre
tip the salad can be arranged on a platter several hours ahead, cover and refrigerate until required. Add the dressing and the toasted pecans just before serving.

Shaved fennel and parmesan salad

6 baby fennel bulbs (900g), trimmed
100g parmesan cheese
¼ cup loosely packed fennel tops
lemon vinaigrette
¼ cup (60ml) olive oil
2 tablespoons lemon juice
2 teaspoons finely chopped fennel tops
1 clove garlic, crushed
1 teaspoon dijon mustard
1 teaspoon white sugar

1 Using a mandolin, v-slicer or sharp knife, slice fennel thinly. Using a vegetable peeler, peel flakes from cheese.
2 Make lemon vinaigrette.
3 Place fennel, cheese and fennel tops in large bowl with vinaigrette; toss gently to combine.
lemon vinaigrette place ingredients in screw-top jar; shake well.

on the table in 15 minutes
serves 6 as an accompaniment **per serving** 14.6g total fat (4.7g saturated fat); 752kJ (180 cal); 3.7g carbohydrate; 7.3g protein; 2.5g fibre
tip lemon vinaigrette can be made a day ahead. Assemble the salad close to serving.

Vegetable, bean and basil salad

340g asparagus, trimmed, cut into 4cm lengths
150g snow peas, trimmed, halved diagonally
1 small red oak leaf lettuce, torn
400g can white beans, rinsed, drained
250g cherry tomatoes, halved
200g fetta cheese, crumbled
1 cup loosely packed fresh baby basil leaves
basil dressing
2 tablespoons finely chopped fresh basil
¼ cup (60ml) olive oil
2 tablespoons white wine vinegar
1 tablespoon lemon juice
1 teaspoon dijon mustard

1 Boil, steam or microwave asparagus and snow peas, separately, until just tender; drain. Rinse under cold water; drain.
2 Make basil dressing.
3 Arrange lettuce on platter; top with asparagus, snow peas and beans, drizzle with a quarter of the dressing. Arrange tomato, cheese and basil on top; drizzle with remaining dressing.
basil dressing place ingredients in screw-top jar; shake well.

on the table in 15 minutes
serves 6 **per serving** 17.2g total fat (6.4g saturated fat); 878kJ (210 cal); 4.3g carbohydrate; 9.5g protein; 3.7g fibre
tip many varieties of already cooked white beans are available canned, among them cannellini, butter and haricot beans; any of these is suitable for this salad.

Moroccan-style carrot and orange salad

500g small carrots, peeled
2 small oranges (360g), peeled, segmented
½ small red onion (40g), sliced
¼ cup loosely packed fresh coriander leaves
1 tablespoon orange flower water
2 tablespoons caster sugar
2 tablespoons lemon juice

1 Cut carrots into thin strips.
2 Combine carrots and remaining ingredients in large bowl.

on the table in 20 minutes
serves 6 **per serving** 0.1g total fat (0.0g saturated fat); 230kJ (55 cal);
10.6g carbohydrate; 1.2g protein; 3.1g fibre
tip there are several different brands of orange flower water available,
all with varying potency. Start with half the quantity stated in the recipe,
taste, then add more if required.

Baby spinach and haloumi salad

340g asparagus, trimmed, cut into 5cm lengths
250g haloumi cheese, sliced thinly
2 large avocados (640g), sliced thinly
200g baby spinach leaves
4 green onions, sliced thinly
chive dressing
¼ cup (60ml) olive oil
2 tablespoons lemon juice
2 teaspoons finely chopped fresh chives

1 Boil, steam or microwave asparagus until tender; drain. Rinse under cold water; drain.
2 Heat large oiled frying pan; cook cheese, in batches, until browned lightly both sides.
3 Make chive dressing.
4 Place asparagus and cheese in large bowl with remaining ingredients and dressing; toss gently to combine.
chive dressing place ingredients in screw-top jar; shake well.

on the table in 25 minutes
serves 4 **per serving** 49.9g total fat (14.3g saturated fat); 2207kJ (528 cal); 3.2g carbohydrate; 17.9g protein; 3.9g fibre

White bean, corn and avocado salad

400g can cannellini beans, rinsed, drained
310g can corn kernels, rinsed, drained
2 trimmed celery stalks (200g), sliced
100g roasted capsicums, chopped
1 large avocado (250g), chopped
chive dressing
2 tablespoons chopped fresh chives
1 tablespoon olive oil
1 tablespoon lemon juice
1 tablespoon red wine vinegar

1 Make chive dressing.
2 Place beans, corn, celery, capsicum and avocado in large bowl with dressing; toss gently to combine.
chive dressing place ingredients in screw-top jar; shake well.

on the table in 15 minutes
serves 6 **per serving** 11.5g total fat (2.0g saturated fat); 782kJ (187 cal); 13.5g carbohydrate; 4.9g protein; 5.0g fibre
tip chive dressing, without the chives, can be prepared a day ahead. Add chives and toss through the salad just before serving.

Burghul salad with chickpeas

1 large red capsicum (350g)
1 cup (160g) burghul
1 cup (250ml) boiling water
420g can chickpeas, rinsed, drained
1 trimmed celery stalk (100g), chopped finely
50g baby spinach leaves
sumac and herb dressing
1 tablespoon sesame seeds
2 tablespoons sumac
1 tablespoon fresh thyme leaves
1 tablespoon coarsely chopped fresh oregano
½ cup (125ml) lime juice
1 tablespoon olive oil
1 clove garlic, crushed

1 Quarter capsicum; discard seeds and membranes. Roast under grill
or in very hot oven [240°C/220°C fan-forced], skin-side up, until skin
blisters and blackens. Cover capsicum pieces with plastic or paper for
5 minutes; peel away skin, then slice capsicum thinly.
2 Place burghul in medium bowl, cover with the boiling water; stand
about 10 minutes or until burghul softens and water is absorbed.
3 Make sumac and herb dressing.
4 Place burghul and capsicum in large bowl with chickpeas, celery,
spinach and dressing; toss gently.
sumac and herb dressing place ingredients in screw-top jar; shake well.

on the table in 30 minutes
serves 4 **per serving** 8.6g total fat (1.2g saturated fat); 1150kJ (275 cal);
37.3g carbohydrate; 11.2g protein; 11.8g fibre

Salad of asian greens

1 small wombok (700g), sliced thinly
1 red oak leaf lettuce (380g), torn
100g mizuna
100g snow pea sprouts, trimmed
100g snow peas, trimmed, sliced thinly
½ small white radish (200g), sliced thinly
4 green onions, sliced thinly
sesame and ginger dressing
⅓ cup (80ml) salt-reduced soy sauce
2 tablespoons white vinegar
2 teaspoons sesame oil
1cm piece fresh ginger (5g), grated
1 clove garlic, crushed

1 Make sesame and ginger dressing.
2 Place ingredients in large bowl with dressing; toss gently to combine.
sesame and ginger dressing place ingredients in screw-top jar;
shake well.

on the table in 20 minutes
serves 8 **per serving** 1.4g total fat (0.2g saturated fat); 192 kJ (46 cal);
4.8g carbohydrate; 3.2g protein; 3.1g fibre

Stuffed zucchini flowers and radicchio salad

Buy zucchini flowers with the tiny young vegetable attached if possible. You need to buy two radicchio for this recipe; use only the inner leaves and hearts, discarding the tough outer leaves. We used a firm goat cheese for this recipe; if you can only find a soft version of this cheese, crumble rather than grate it.

2 tablespoons finely chopped fresh sage
2 teaspoons finely grated lemon rind
1 small red onion (100g), chopped finely
100g firm goat cheese, grated coarsely
100g ricotta cheese
24 small zucchini (700g) with flowers attached
250g yellow teardrop tomatoes
1 tablespoon olive oil
1 teaspoon balsamic vinegar
100g radicchio leaves, torn

1 Preheat oven to 240°C/220°C fan-forced.
2 Place sage, rind, onion and cheeses in small bowl; beat with wooden spoon until combined.
3 Remove and discard stamens from centre of flowers; fill flowers with cheese mixture, twist petal tops to enclose filling. Place filled flowers on lightly oiled oven tray. Place tomatoes, in single layer, in small shallow baking dish; drizzle with combined oil and vinegar. Roast flowers and tomatoes, both uncovered, about 10 minutes or until flowers are browned lightly and heated through, and tomatoes are softened.
4 Toss tomatoes and pan juices in medium bowl with radicchio; serve with zucchini flowers.

on the table in 35 minutes
serves 4 **per serving** 11.8g total fat (5.0g saturated fat); 711kJ (170 cal); 5.5g carbohydrate; 8.3g protein; 3.8g fibre
tip you can use a piping bag fitted with a large plain tube to pipe filling into the zucchini flowers.

Sesame omelette and crisp mixed vegetable salad

You will need about half a medium wombok for this recipe.

8 eggs
½ cup (125ml) milk
½ cup coarsely chopped fresh garlic chives
2 tablespoons toasted sesame seeds
8 cups (640g) finely shredded wombok
2 fresh long red chillies, sliced thinly
1 large red capsicum (350g), sliced thinly
1 large green capsicum (350g), sliced thinly
1 tablespoon coarsely chopped fresh mint
5cm stick (10g) fresh lemon grass, chopped finely
sweet chilli dressing
2 teaspoons toasted sesame seeds
¼ cup (60ml) rice vinegar
¼ cup (60ml) peanut oil
1 teaspoon sesame oil
¼ cup (60ml) sweet chilli sauce

1 Whisk eggs in large jug with milk, chives and seeds until well combined. Pour a quarter of the egg mixture into heated lightly oiled wok; cook over medium heat, tilting pan, until omelette is just set. Remove from wok; repeat with remaining egg mixture to make four omelettes. Roll cooled omelettes tightly; cut into 3mm "wheels".
2 Make sweet chilli dressing.
3 Place three-quarters of the omelette in large bowl with wombok, chilli, capsicums, mint, lemon grass and dressing; toss gently to combine. Divide salad among serving plates; top with remaining omelette.
sweet chilli dressing place ingredients in screw-top jar; shake well.

on the table in 35 minutes
serves 4 **per serving** 31.1g total fat (7.2g saturated fat); 1726kJ (413 cal); 11.1g carbohydrate; 20.2g protein; 5.2g fibre
tip omelettes can be made up to 3 hours ahead and stored, covered, in the refrigerator; roll and slice just before assembling salad.

Fetta, bean and potato salad

2 x 360g packets fresh baby potatoes with butter and parsley
250g baby beans
4 medium tomatoes (500g), chopped
200g fetta cheese, chopped
2 tablespoons baby capers, rinsed, drained
1 cup (200g) black olives
dressing
¼ cup (60ml) white wine vinegar
¾ cup (180ml) olive oil
1 teaspoon dijon mustard
1 tablespoon finely chopped fresh chives

1 Boil, steam or microwave potatoes until just tender.
2 Make dressing.
3 Toss potatoes with half of the dressing.
4 Boil, steam or microwave beans until just tender; drain.
5 Place potatoes, beans, tomatoes, cheese, capers and olives in large
bowl with remaining dressing; toss gently to combine.
dressing place ingredients in screw-top jar; shake well.

on the table in 25 minutes
serves 4 **per serving** 46.1g total fat (8.6g saturated fat); 2579kJ (617 cal);
39.6g carbohydrate; 7.5g protein; 7.6g fibre

Coleslaw

This is a perfect coleslaw for people who don't care for creamy salad dressings.

1 medium white cabbage (1.5kg), shredded finely
15 green onions, chopped finely
2 fresh small red thai chillies, chopped finely
1 cup coarsely chopped fresh mint
½ cup coarsely chopped fresh flat-leaf parsley
¼ cup coarsely chopped fresh coriander
lemon dressing
¼ cup (60ml) lemon juice
1 tablespoon dijon mustard
½ cup (125ml) peanut oil

1 Combine cabbage in large bowl with onion, chilli and herbs.
2 Make lemon dressing.
3 Pour dressing over salad; toss to combine.
lemon dressing place ingredients in screw-top jar; shake well.

on the table in 20 minutes
serves 8 **per serving** 14.6g total fat (2.6g saturated fat); 773kJ (185 cal); 6.8g carbohydrate; 3.2g protein; 8.3g fibre

Zucchini ribbon salad with spearmint and almonds

There are many varieties of mint, but one of the most common is the grey-green spearmint with its mild flavour and delicate aroma. It grows wild in many of our gardens during summer but your greengrocer should be able to obtain it for you all year long.

4 medium green zucchini (480g)
4 medium yellow zucchini (480g)
½ cup (80g) blanched almonds, toasted
2 large red capsicums (700g), sliced thinly
⅓ cup finely chopped fresh spearmint
raspberry vinaigrette
½ cup (125ml) olive oil
1 tablespoon lemon juice
1 teaspoon finely grated lemon rind
2 tablespoons raspberry vinegar

1 Using vegetable peeler, cut zucchini into thin ribbons.
2 Make raspberry vinaigrette.
3 Place zucchini in large bowl with almonds, capsicum, mint and vinaigrette; toss gently to combine.
raspberry vinaigrette place ingredients in screw-top jar; shake well.

on the table in 20 minutes
serves 6 **per serving** 27.0g total fat (3.2g saturated fat); 1275kJ (305 cal); 7.3g carbohydrate; 6.3g protein; 5.1g fibre
tip select mint leaves that are evenly coloured and have no brown tinge around the edges. A bunch of mint can be kept, stems in a jar of water and leaves covered with a plastic bag, in the refrigerator, up to 5 days.

Avocado caesar salad

2 small white bread rolls (80g), sliced thinly
1 clove garlic, crushed
1 tablespoon olive oil
2 baby cos lettuce, torn
1 large red onion (300g), sliced thinly
2 medium avocados (500g), chopped coarsely
⅓ cup (50g) sun-dried tomatoes in oil, drained, sliced thinly
60g parmesan cheese, shaved
dressing
1 clove garlic, crushed
2 egg yolks
2 teaspoons dijon mustard
2 tablespoons white vinegar
1 cup (250ml) extra light olive oil

1 Preheat oven to 200°C/180°C fan-forced.
2 Place bread slices, in single layer, on oven tray; brush with combined garlic and oil. Toast in oven about 5 minutes or until crisp.
3 Make dressing.
4 Place toast in large bowl with remaining ingredients and dressing; toss gently to combine.
dressing blend or process garlic, yolks, mustard and vinegar until smooth. With motor operating, gradually add oil in a thin steady stream; process until mixture thickens.

on the table in 25 minutes
serves 4 **per serving** 90.4g total fat (17.1g saturated fat); 3984kJ (953 cal); 19.7g carbohydrate; 14.5g protein; 6.9g fibre
tip garlic toasts can be made a day ahead; store in an airtight container.

Baby beet salad

850g can whole baby beets, rinsed, drained, quartered
1 cup (80g) bean sprouts
1 medium carrot (120g), sliced thinly
1 trimmed celery stalk (100g), sliced thinly
1 small red onion (100g), sliced thinly
½ cup loosely packed fresh mint leaves
dressing
1 tablespoon finely grated lime rind
¼ cup (60ml) lime juice
2 tablespoons olive oil

1 Make dressing.
2 Place beets, sprouts, carrot, celery, onion and mint in large serving bowl with dressing; toss gently to combine.
dressing place ingredients in screw-top jar; shake well.

on the table in 20 minutes
serves 4 **per serving** 9.4g total fat (1.3g saturated fat); 752kJ (180 cal); 17.5g carbohydrate; 3.6g protein; 6.4g fibre

Rocket salad

200g rocket or lettuce leaves
1 small red onion (100g), sliced thinly
dressing
2 tablespoons olive oil
1 tablespoon red or white wine vinegar
½ teaspoon dijon mustard
½ teaspoon white sugar

1 Make dressing.
2 Place rocket and onion in large serving bowl with dressing; toss gently to combine.
dressing place ingredients in screw-top jar; shake well.

on the table in 5 minutes
serves 6 **per serving** 6.3g total fat (0.9g saturated fat); 293kJ (70 cal); 2.0g carbohydrate; 1.1g protein; 0.7g fibre
tip rocket has a peppery flavour; you may prefer to substitute your favourite lettuce variety.

Salade composé

Literally meaning "composed salad", the ingredients in this dish are layered on top of each other, rather than being tossed together, and the dressing is drizzled over the top.

1 small french bread stick
2 cloves garlic, crushed
¼ cup (60ml) olive oil
6 bacon rashers (420g), rind removed, sliced thickly
150g mesclun
6 medium egg tomatoes (450g), sliced thinly
4 hard-boiled eggs, halved lengthways
red wine vinaigrette
¼ cup (60ml) red wine vinegar
3 teaspoons dijon mustard
⅓ cup (80ml) olive oil

1 Preheat grill.
2 Cut bread into 1cm slices. Brush both sides with combined garlic and oil; toast under preheated grill.
3 Cook bacon in large frying pan until crisp; drain on absorbent paper.
4 Make red wine vinaigrette.
5 Layer bread and bacon in large bowl with mesclun and tomato, top with egg; drizzle with vinaigrette.
red wine vinaigrette place ingredients in screw-top jar; shake well.

on the table in 35 minutes
serves 4 **per serving** 48.3g total fat (9.9g saturated fat); 2583kJ (618 cal); 19.7g carbohydrate; 25.2g protein; 3.5g fibre

Potato salad with herb vinaigrette

2kg tiny new potatoes, halved
herb vinaigrette
⅓ cup finely chopped fresh mint
⅓ cup finely chopped fresh flat-leaf parsley
⅓ cup (80ml) red wine vinegar
¼ cup (60ml) olive oil
2 tablespoons brown sugar

1 Boil, steam or microwave potato until tender. Drain; keep warm.
2 Make herb vinaigrette.
3 Place potato in large bowl with vinaigrette; toss gently to combine.
herb vinaigrette place ingredients in screw-top jar; shake well.

on the table in 30 minutes
serves 8 **per serving** 7.1g total fat (1.0g saturated fat); 1037kJ (248 cal);
36.2g carbohydrate; 6.1g protein; 5.3g fibre
tip make the vinaigrette a day ahead to allow the flavours to blend; cover,
refrigerate overnight.

Greek salad

6 medium egg tomatoes (450g)
3 lebanese cucumbers (400g)
1 medium green capsicum (200g)
1 small red onion (100g)
1 cup (150g) kalamata olives
½ cup (125ml) olive oil
150g fetta cheese
½ teaspoon crushed dried rigani or oregano

1 Cut tomatoes, cucumber and capsicum into large pieces. Cut onion into wedges.
2 Place tomato, cucumber, capsicum, onion and olives in large serving bowl with almost all of the oil; toss gently to combine.
3 Cut cheese into two large pieces, place on top of salad. Sprinkle with rigani; drizzle with remaining oil.

on the table in 10 minutes
serves 8 **per serving** 18.9g total fat (4.9g saturated fat); 924kJ (221 cal); 7.5g carbohydrate; 4.8g protein; 1.8g fibre
tips dried rigani, similar to oregano but with longer leaves, is found in Greek and Middle-Eastern food shops.

Baby rocket and parmesan salad

This salad is found on the menus of Italian restaurants everywhere in the world. The combination of the rocket's appealing bitterness and the sweet acidity of the balsamic vinegar offer a welcome foil to the richness of many Italian main courses.

60g parmesan cheese
200g baby rocket leaves
80g semi-dried tomatoes, halved lengthways
¼ cup (40g) pine nuts, toasted
¼ cup (60ml) balsamic vinegar
¼ cup (60ml) olive oil

1 Using vegetable peeler, shave cheese into wide, long pieces.
2 Place rocket, tomato and nuts in large bowl with cheese and combined vinegar and oil; toss gently to combine.

on the table in 25 minutes
serves 8 **per serving** 13.4g total fat (2.8g saturated fat); 673kJ (161 cal); 4.1g carbohydrate; 5.2g protein; 2.0g fibre

193

Spinach salad with mushrooms, poached egg and anchovy dressing

40g butter
2 flat mushrooms (200g), sliced thickly
100g swiss brown mushrooms, sliced thickly
100g shiitake mushrooms, sliced thickly
4 eggs
270g char-grilled capsicum in oil, drained, sliced thinly
300g baby spinach leaves
anchovy dressing
2 tablespoons coarsely chopped fresh sage
1 tablespoon drained capers, rinsed
6 anchovy fillets, drained
2 tablespoons balsamic vinegar
¼ cup (60ml) olive oil
2 tablespoons water

1 Melt butter in large frying pan; cook mushrooms, stirring, until tender. Place in large bowl; cover to keep warm.
2 Half-fill a large shallow frying pan with water; bring to a boil. Break eggs into cup, one at a time, then slide into pan. When all eggs are in pan, allow water to return to a boil. Cover pan, turn off heat; stand about 4 minutes or until a light film of egg white sets over yolks. Remove eggs, one at a time, using slotted spoon, and place on absorbent paper-lined plate to blot up poaching liquid.
3 Make anchovy dressing.
4 Add capsicum and half of the dressing to mushroom mixture in large bowl; toss gently to combine.
5 Divide spinach among serving plates; top with mushroom mixture and egg, drizzle with remaining dressing.
anchovy dressing blend or process ingredients until combined.

on the table in 30 minutes
serves 4 **per serving** 26.5g total fat (5.4g saturated fat); 1359kJ (325 cal); 5.4g carbohydrate; 14.4g protein; 4.6g fibre

Vietnamese coleslaw

You will need a wombok weighing approximately 1.2kg for this recipe.

2 medium carrots (240g)
½ small green papaya (325g)
8 cups (640g) coarsely shredded wombok
½ cup firmly packed fresh mint leaves
½ cup firmly packed fresh coriander leaves
½ cup (75g) toasted crushed peanuts
lime dressing
¼ cup (60ml) lime juice
1 clove garlic, crushed
1 fresh small red thai chilli, chopped finely
2 tablespoons grated palm sugar
2 tablespoons fish sauce
2 teaspoons peanut oil

1 Using vegetable peeler, slice carrots and papaya lengthways into ribbons.
2 Make lime dressing.
3 Place carrot and papaya in large bowl with remaining ingredients and dressing; toss gently to combine.
lime dressing place ingredients in screw-top jar; shake well.

on the table in 25 minutes
serves 8 **per serving** 5.7g total fat (0.9g saturated fat); 456kJ (109 cal); 8.6g carbohydrate; 4.2g protein; 3.7g fibre

Tomato, olive and fetta salad

400g grape tomatoes
250g yellow teardrop tomatoes
200g black olives
2 small zucchini (180g), halved lengthways
1 small red onion (80g), sliced thinly
100g fetta cheese, crumbled
dressing
¼ cup (60ml) olive oil
2 tablespoons lemon juice
2 cloves garlic, crushed
1 teaspoon fresh marjoram or oregano leaves

1 Combine tomatoes and olives in medium bowl.
2 Halve zucchini lengthways, then slice thinly on the diagonal. Add zucchini and onion to bowl with tomatoes.
3 Make dressing; pour over salad. Add cheese; toss gently to combine.
dressing place ingredients in screw-top jar; shake well.

on the table in 20 minutes
serves 6 **per serving** 13.6g total fat (3.9g saturated fat); 798kJ (191 cal); 11.4g carbohydrate; 4.4g protein; 3.0g fibre

Potato salad with mustard anchovy dressing

1kg small potatoes, scrubbed
½ cup (120g) sour cream
½ cup (150g) mayonnaise
1 tablespoon dijon mustard
1 anchovy, rinsed, chopped finely
1 clove garlic, crushed
¼ cup fresh flat-leaf parsley leaves
2 teaspoons baby capers, rinsed, drained

1 Boil, steam or microwave potatoes until just tender; drain and cool. Slice potatoes thickly.
2 Combine sour cream, mayonnaise, mustard, anchovies and garlic in large bowl. Gently stir through potatoes and half of the parsley.
3 Serve sprinkled with capers and remaining parsley.

on the table in 35 minutes
serves 4 **per serving** 24.3g total fat (9.3g saturated fat); 1789kJ (428 cal); 41.5g carbohydrate; 7.5g protein; 5.7g fibre
tip this recipe can be made several hours ahead; store, covered, in refrigerator.

Tomato and cucumber salad

½ teaspoon cumin seeds
¼ teaspoon chilli powder
1 medium red onion (170g), sliced thinly
4 medium egg tomatoes (300g), sliced
1 large cucumber (400g), sliced thinly
2 tablespoons lemon juice

1 Dry-fry cumin seeds in small frying pan, stirring, over low heat until fragrant. Blend, process or pound (using a pestle and mortar) cumin seeds and chilli powder until finely crushed.
2 Combine spice mixture and onion in small bowl.
3 Arrange tomato slices on a plate; top with cucumber. Drizzle with juice and top with onion mixture.

on the table in 15 minutes
serves 8 **per serving** 0.1g total fat (0.0g saturated fat); 84kJ (20 cal); 3.0g carbohydrate; 1.0g protein; 1.0g fibre
tip the spices can be prepared several hours ahead. The recipe is best assembled close to serving.

Lamb's lettuce, avocado and tomato salad

Lamb's lettuce, also known as mâche or corn salad, has a mild, almost nutty flavour and tender, narrow, dark-green leaves.

60g lamb's lettuce
250g yellow teardrop tomatoes, halved
250g cherry tomatoes, halved
1 small red onion (100g), sliced thinly
1 medium avocado (250g), chopped coarsely
¼ cup coarsely chopped fresh flat-leaf parsley
1 tablespoon finely shredded fresh basil
dressing
¼ cup (60ml) olive oil
2 tablespoons balsamic vinegar
1 teaspoon brown sugar
1 clove garlic, crushed

1 Make dressing.
2 Place lamb's lettuce, tomatoes, onion, avocado and herbs in large serving bowl with dressing; toss gently to combine.
dressing place ingredients in screw-top jar; shake well.

on the table in 15 minutes
serves 4 **per serving** 23.7g total fat (4.1g saturated fat); 1041kJ (249 cal); 5.2g carbohydrate; 2.1g protein; 3.6g fibre

Bitter lettuce salad

1 small radicchio lettuce
100g curly endive
1 large bunch chicory
⅓ cup (80ml) olive oil
2 tablespoons red wine vinegar

1 Trim lettuce, endive and chicory leaves; wash and dry well.
2 Place salad leaves in large bowl with combined oil and vinegar; toss gently to combine.

on the table in 10 minutes
serves 8 **per serving** 9.2g total fat (1.3g saturated fat); 368kJ (88 cal); 0.4g carbohydrate; 0.6g protein; 0.9g fibre

Greek spring salad

1 large cos lettuce, shredded finely
6 green onions, sliced thinly
2 tablespoons chopped fresh dill
dressing
⅓ cup (80ml) olive oil
1½ tablespoons red wine vinegar

1 Make dressing.
2 Place lettuce, onion and dill in large serving bowl with dressing;
toss gently to combine.
dressing place ingredients in screw-top jar; shake well.

on the table in 10 minutes
serves 8 **per serving** 9.4g total fat (1.3g saturated fat); 431kJ (103 cal);
2.1g carbohydrate; 1.5g protein; 2.3g fibre
tip this salad can be prepared three hours ahead; add the dressing just
before serving.

Tabbouleh

Made with fresh parsley, mint and burghul (crushed processed wheat kernels), tabbouleh is a cornerstone of Middle-Eastern cuisine. You will need about three bunches of flat-leaf parsley for this recipe.

½ cup (80g) burghul
3 cups coarsely chopped fresh flat-leaf parsley
3 medium tomatoes (450g), chopped finely
1 small red onion (100g), chopped finely
1 cup coarsely chopped fresh mint
½ cup (125ml) lemon juice
¼ cup (60ml) olive oil

1 Cover burghul with water in small bowl; stand about 10 minutes or until burghul softens. Drain in fine strainer; squeeze out excess liquid.
2 Place burghul in large bowl with parsley, tomato, onion, mint and combined juice and oil; toss gently to combine.

on the table in 25 minutes
serves 4 **per serving** 14.4g total fat (2.0g saturated fat); 991kJ (237 cal); 17.0g carbohydrate; 5.1g protein; 8.1g fibre

Broad bean salad with anchovy dressing

1kg frozen broad beans, thawed
½ cup coarsely chopped fresh chives
1 medium red onion (170g), chopped finely
anchoy dressing
8 anchovy fillets, drained
⅓ cup (80ml) lemon juice
⅓ cup (80ml) olive oil
2 cloves garlic, quartered
2 teaspoons drained bottled capers

1 Boil, steam or microwave beans until just tender; drain. Rinse immediately under cold water to stop cooking process; drain. Peel away and discard outer beige shell.
2 Make anchoy dressing.
3 Place beans in large bowl with chives, onion and dressing; toss gently to combine.
anchovy dressing blend or process ingredients until smooth.

on the table in 35 minutes
serves 6 **per serving** 13.0g total fat (1.8g saturated fat); 1058kJ (253 cal); 16.0g carbohydrate; 10.9g protein; 14.4g fibre
tip if fresh broad beans are in season, use them rather than the frozen variety. You will need to buy 1.5kg fresh broad beans in their pods; shell before cooking until just tender.

Rocket and macadamia salad

750g asparagus, trimmed, halved
200g baby rocket leaves
1 large avocado (320g), sliced thinly
½ cup (75g) macadamia nuts, toasted, chopped coarsely
2 tablespoons sherry vinegar
¼ cup (60ml) macadamia or olive oil

1 Barbecue or grill asparagus, in batches, until just tender; cool.
2 Combine asparagus on serving platter with rocket, avocado and nuts.
3 Drizzle with combined vinegar and oil.

on the table in 15 minutes
serves 8 **per serving** 20.6g total fat (3.3g saturated fat); 878kJ (210 cal);
2.0g carbohydrate; 3.5g protein; 2.3g fibre

stir-fry

Asian greens with kaffir lime rice

1 litre (4 cups) cold water
2 cups (400g) jasmine rice
4 fresh kaffir lime leaves, shredded
4cm piece fresh ginger (20g), chopped coarsely
2 fresh long red chillies, chopped coarsely
1 tablespoon sesame oil
1 large brown onion (200g), sliced thickly
200g green beans, trimmed
300g baby buk choy, quartered lengthways
100g snow peas, trimmed
150g oyster mushrooms, halved
100g enoki mushrooms, trimmed
¼ cup (80ml) lime juice
2 tablespoons soy sauce
¼ cup coarsely chopped fresh coriander

1 Combine the water, rice, lime leaves, ginger and chilli in large saucepan with a tight-fitting lid; bring to a boil. Reduce heat, cook, covered, about 12 minutes or until all water is absorbed and rice is cooked. Do not remove lid or stir rice during cooking time. Remove from heat; stand, covered, 10 minutes before serving.
2 Heat half of the oil in wok; stir-fry onion until just softened. Add beans; stir-fry until just tender. Add buk choy, snow peas and mushrooms; stir-fry until buk choy just wilts. Add juice, sauce, coriander and remaining oil; stir-fry to combine.
3 Serve stir-fry with rice.

on the table in 35 minutes
serves 4 **per serving** 5.7g total fat (0.8g saturated fat); 1889kJ (452 cal); 85.7g carbohydrate; 12.9g protein; 7g fibre

Stir-fried cauliflower, choy sum and snake beans

You will need about 1kg cauliflower for this recipe.

1 tablespoon peanut oil
2 cloves garlic, crushed
1 teaspoon ground turmeric
1 teaspoon finely chopped coriander root and stem mixture
4 green onions, sliced thinly
500g cauliflower florets
¼ cup (60ml) water
200g snake beans, cut into 5cm pieces
200g choy sum, chopped coarsely
1 tablespoon lime juice
1 tablespoon soy sauce
1 tablespoon finely chopped fresh coriander

1 Heat oil in wok; cook garlic, turmeric, coriander mixture and onion; stir-fry until onion just softens. Remove from wok; keep warm.
2 Stir-fry cauliflower with the water in wok until cauliflower is almost tender. Add beans and choy sum; stir-fry until vegetables are just tender.
3 Add juice, sauce, chopped coriander and onion mixture; stir-fry until heated through.

on the table in 30 minutes
serves 4 **per serving** 5.0g total fat (0.8g saturated fat); 380kJ (91 cal); 4.3g carbohydrate; 5.0g protein; 4.2g fibre
tip both the stems and roots of coriander are used in this recipe so buy a bunch of fresh coriander with its roots intact. Wash the coriander under cold water, removing any dirt clinging to the roots. Chop roots and stems together and some of the leaves for the tablespoon specified. Freeze the remainder of the chopped root and stem mixture, in teaspoon-size plastic-wrap parcels, for future use.

Vegetable chap-chai

1 tablespoon peanut oil
1 clove garlic, crushed
4cm piece fresh ginger (20g), grated finely
300g pak choy, trimmed
500g choy sum, chopped coarsely
400g baby buk choy, chopped coarsely
450g wombok, chopped coarsely
1 tablespoon soy sauce
½ cup (60ml) hoisin sauce
1 tablespoon plum sauce
2 teaspoons sambal oelek
1½ cups (120g) bean sprouts

1 Heat oil in wok; stir-fry garlic and ginger until fragrant.
2 Add pak choy, choy sum, buk choy, wombok, combined sauces and sambal oelek; stir-fry until vegetables are just tender.
3 Add sprouts; stir-fry, tossing until sprouts just wilt.

on the table in 30 minutes
serves 4 **per serving** 6.2g total fat (1.0g saturated fat); 656kJ (157 cal); 15.1g carbohydrate; 6.1g protein; 8.4g fibre

Stir-fried gai lan

1kg gai lan, trimmed, chopped coarsely
1 tablespoon peanut oil
5 green onions, chopped coarsely
2 cloves garlic, crushed
2cm piece fresh ginger (10g), grated finely
2 tablespoons soy sauce
2 tablespoons oyster sauce
1 tablespoon fish sauce
¼ cup (60ml) keçap manis
2 tablespoons sesame seeds

1 Boil, steam or microwave gai lan until just tender; drain.
2 Heat oil in wok; stir-fry onion, garlic and ginger until fragrant. Add gai lan and sauces; stir until heated through. Drizzle with keçap manis; toss with sesame seeds.

on the table in 20 minutes
serves 4 **per serving** 28.1g total fat (5.3g saturated fat); 1668kJ (399 cal); 22.0g carbohydrate; 12.3g protein; 6.5g fibre

Pumpkin, basil and chilli stir-fry

⅓ cup (80ml) peanut oil
1 large brown onion (200g), sliced thinly
2 cloves garlic, sliced thinly
4 fresh small red thai chillies, sliced thinly
1kg pumpkin, chopped coarsely
250g sugar snap peas
1 teaspoon grated palm sugar
¼ cup (60ml) vegetable stock
2 tablespoons soy sauce
¾ cup loosely packed opal basil leaves
4 green onions, sliced thinly
½ cup (75g) roasted unsalted peanuts

1 Heat oil in wok; cook brown onion until browned and crisp. Drain on absorbent paper.
2 Stir-fry garlic and chilli in wok until fragrant. Add pumpkin; stir-fry until browned all over and just tender. Add peas, sugar, stock and sauce; stir-fry until sauce thickens slightly.
3 Remove from heat; toss basil, green onion and nuts through stir-fry until well combined. Serve topped with fried onion.

on the table in 25 minutes
serves 4 **per serving** 28.1g total fat (5.3g saturated fat); 1668kJ (399 cal); 22.0g carbohydrate; 12.3g protein; 6.5g fibre

Asian greens in oyster sauce

1 cup (250ml) chicken stock
⅓ cup (80ml) oyster sauce
2 teaspoons sesame oil
2kg baby buk choy, trimmed
1kg choy sum, trimmed

1 Combine stock, sauce and oil in wok; bring mixture to a boil.
2 Add buk choy; cook, stirring, about 3 minutes or until buk choy is slightly wilted.
3 Stir in choy sum; cook, covered, about 5 minutes or until both greens are tender and just wilted.

on the table in 15 minutes
serves 6 **per serving** 2.8g total fat (0.3g saturated fat); 422kJ (101 cal); 8.7g carbohydrate; 6.4g protein; 6.5g fibre
tip use any leafy green asian vegetables you like in this recipe but be certain that you prepare the recipe just before serving.

Snow pea stir-fry with sesame seeds and pine nuts

1 tablespoon sesame oil
600g snow peas, trimmed
2 green onions, sliced thinly
2 tablespoons toasted pine nuts
1 tablespoon toasted sesame seeds

1 Heat oil in wok; stir-fry snow peas and onion until snow peas are just tender.
2 Add nuts and seeds to wok; stir-fry briefly to combine.

on the table in 15 minutes
serves 4 **per serving** 9.9g total fat (1.0g saturated fat); 594kJ (142 cal); 6.9g carbohydrate; 5.1g protein; 3.6g fibre

Fried tofu and green vegetables

We used packaged fried tofu which you can buy from many supermarkets. However, if you prefer to do it yourself, you can shallow-fry cubes of firm tofu in vegetable oil until browned lightly, then drain on absorbent paper.

1 tablespoon peanut oil
1 large brown onion (200g), sliced thickly
2 cloves garlic, crushed
4cm piece fresh ginger (20g), grated finely
2 fresh small red thai chillies, chopped finely
200g green beans
250g asparagus
500g baby buk choy, quartered
500g choy sum, chopped coarsely
1 tablespoon fish sauce
2 tablespoons sweet chilli sauce
2 tablespoons brown sugar
¼ cup (60ml) lime juice
300g fried tofu
¼ cup finely chopped fresh coriander
¼ cup finely chopped fresh mint

1 Heat oil in wok; stir-fry onion, garlic, ginger and chilli until onion just softens.
2 Add beans and asparagus to wok; stir-fry until tender.
3 Add buk choy, choy sum, sauces, sugar and juice; stir-fry until buk choy just wilts. Add tofu and herbs; stir-fry until hot.

on the table in 30 minutes
serves 4 **per serving** 10.8g total fat (1.6g saturated fat); 1024kJ (245 cal); 17.3g carbohydrate; 15.5g protein; 8.5g fibre

Stir-fried vegetables with rice noodles

You will need about 300g broccoli for this recipe.

250g dried rice noodles
1 tablespoon peanut oil
1 teaspoon sesame oil
1 large brown onion (200g), sliced thickly
1 clove garlic, crushed
¼ cup (60ml) light soy sauce
⅓ cup (80ml) sweet chilli sauce
½ cup (125ml) water
2cm piece fresh ginger (10g), grated finely
1 tablespoon sweet sherry
2 teaspoons cornflour
2 tablespoons water, extra
1 medium red capsicum (200g), chopped coarsely
180g broccoli florets
150g snow peas, halved lengthways
425g can baby corn cuts, drained, halved lengthways

1 Place noodles in medium heatproof bowl, cover with boiling water, stand until tender; drain.
2 Heat oils in wok; stir-fry onion and garlic until onion softens. Add sauces, the water, ginger and sherry; bring to a boil. Blend cornflour and the extra water, add to wok; stir until sauce boils and thickens.
3 Add capsicum, broccoli, snow peas and corn; stir-fry until vegetables are just tender.
4 Serve noodles with stir-fried vegetables.

on the table in 25 minutes
serves 4 **per serving** 7.4g total fat (1.1g saturated fat); 1346kJ (322 cal); 47.9g carbohydrate; 10.0g protein; 8.5g fibre

Stir-fried mushrooms and kang kong

8 dried shiitake mushrooms
1 tablespoon peanut oil
2 cloves garlic, crushed
1cm piece fresh ginger (5g), grated finely
400g oyster mushrooms, halved
400g button mushrooms, quartered
425g can straw mushrooms, drained
900g kang kong, shredded
5 green onions, sliced thinly
1 tablespoon light soy sauce
1 tablespoon mild sweet chilli sauce
1 tablespoon oyster sauce
1 tablespoon rice vinegar

1 Place dried mushrooms in small heatproof bowl; cover with boiling water. Stand 20 minutes; drain. Discard stems; slice caps.
2 Heat oil in wok; stir-fry garlic, ginger and mushrooms 1 minute. Add kang kong, onion and combined sauces and vinegar; stir-fry until kang kong just wilts.

on the table in 35 minutes
serves 6 **per serving** 4.5g total fat (0.7g saturated fat); 543kJ (130 cal); 5.4g carbohydrate; 11.2g protein; 11.0g fibre

Stir-fried asian greens in black bean sauce

2 cups (400g) jasmine rice
1 tablespoon peanut oil
150g sugar snap peas, trimmed
400g gai lan, chopped coarsely
200g snake beans, trimmed, cut into 5cm lengths
2 cloves garlic, sliced thinly
1 fresh small red thai chilli, chopped finely
2 medium zucchini (240g), sliced thickly
2 tablespoons black bean sauce
1 tablespoon kecap manis
1 teaspoon sesame oil
1/3 cup (50g) toasted unsalted cashews, chopped coarsely

1 Cook rice in large saucepan of boiling water, uncovered, until just tender; drain.
2 Heat peanut oil in wok; stir-fry peas, gai lan stems, beans, garlic, chilli and zucchini until stems are just tender.
3 Add sauces, sesame oil, gai lan leaves and nuts; stir-fry until leaves are just wilted.
4 Serve stir-fry with rice.

on the table in 25 minutes
serves 4 **per serving** 13.3g total fat (2.6g saturated fat); 2274kJ (544 cal); 89.5g carbohydrate; 15.4g protein; 8.8g fibre

pan-fry

Zucchini with chorizo

1 fresh chorizo sausage (160g)
4 medium zucchini (480g), sliced

1 Squeeze filling from sausage casing. Cook sausage in large heated frying pan, stirring, until sausage browns and crumbles. Remove from pan; retain oil in pan.
2 Add zucchini to same pan; cook, stirring, until browned and tender.
3 Return sausage to pan; cook, stirring, until combined.

on the table in 20 minutes
serves 8 **per serving** 6.2g total fat (2.2g saturated fat); 339kJ (81 cal); 1.5g carbohydrate; 4.6g protein; 1.0g fibre
tip if fresh chorizo is unavailable, substitute sliced semi-dried chorizo (salami-style).

Bow ties with zucchini in lemon garlic sauce

375g bow tie pasta
3 medium green zucchini (360g)
3 medium yellow zucchini (360g)
30g butter
1 tablespoon olive oil
2 cloves garlic, crushed
⅓ cup (80ml) vegetable stock
½ cup (125ml) cream
2 teaspoons finely grated lemon rind
⅓ cup coarsely chopped fresh chives

1 Cook pasta in large saucepan of boiling water, uncovered, until just tender; drain.
2 Halve zucchini lengthways; slice halves thinly on the diagonal.
3 Heat butter and oil in large frying pan; cook zucchini and garlic over high heat, stirring, until zucchini is just tender. Add stock; bring to a boil. Reduce heat, add cream, rind and chives; stir until hot.
4 Add pasta to pan with zucchini sauce; toss gently to combine.

on the table in 30 minutes
serves 4 **per serving** 25.9g total fat (13.9g saturated fat); 2408kJ (576 cal); 67.7g carbohydrate; 14.6g protein; 6.4g fibre

Garlic mushrooms

90g butter
3 cloves garlic, crushed
750g button mushrooms
1 tablespoon lemon juice
2 tablespoons coarsely chopped fresh flat-leaf parsley

1 Melt butter in large frying pan; cook garlic, stirring, about 1 minute or until fragrant.
2 Add mushrooms to pan, stir to coat in butter mixture; cook, covered, over high heat, stirring occasionally, until mushrooms are almost tender. Remove lid; bring to a boil. Boil until liquid is reduced by half and mushrooms are tender.
3 Stir in juice and parsley

on the table in 20 minutes
serves 8 as a starter **per serving** 9.5g total fat (6.1g saturated fat); 464kJ (111 cal); 1.7g carbohydrate; 3.6g protein; 2.6g fibre

Cauliflower and broccoli curry

1 tablespoon peanut oil
2 tablespoons red curry paste
1 large red capsicum (350g), sliced thinly
1 tablespoon honey
3⅓ cups (830ml) coconut cream
1 cup (250ml) water
500g broccoli, chopped coarsely
500g cauliflower, chopped coarsely
425g can whole baby corn spears, drained
500g choy sum, chopped coarsely

1 Heat oil in large deep frying pan; cook paste, stirring, until fragrant.
Add capsicum; cook, stirring, until almost tender.
2 Stir in honey, coconut cream and the water; bring to a boil. Add broccoli
and cauliflower, reduce heat; simmer, uncovered, 2 minutes.
3 Add corn and choy sum; cook, stirring, until choy sum just wilts.

on the table in 35 minutes
serves 4 **per serving** 52.1g total fat (38.9g saturated fat); 2692kJ
(644 cal); 23.6g carbohydrate; 14.9g protein; 15.5g fibre
tip different brands of commercially prepared curry pastes vary in
strength and flavour, so you may want to adjust the amount of paste
to suit your taste.

Moroccan-style vegetables with couscous

2 tablespoons olive oil
2 large white onions (400g), sliced thickly
2 cloves garlic, crushed
2 teaspoons ground coriander
1 teaspoon ground cumin
1 teaspoon sweet paprika
2 cinnamon sticks
pinch ground saffron
2 fresh small red thai chillies, finely chopped
2 finger eggplant (120g), chopped coarsely
80g peeled pumpkin, chopped
400g can chopped tomatoes
1 cup (250ml) vegetable stock
2 cups (500ml) water
300g can chickpeas, rinsed, drained
2 large zucchini (300g), chopped coarsely
½ cup loosely packed fresh coriander leaves
1 tablespoon lemon juice
couscous
1 cup (250ml) vegetable stock
1 cup (250ml) water
60g butter
1½ cups (300g) couscous

1 Heat oil in large, deep frying pan; cook onion and garlic, stirring, until onion is soft. Add spices, chilli and eggplant; cook, stirring, until fragrant.
2 Add pumpkin, undrained tomatoes, stock, water and chickpeas, bring to a boil; simmer, covered, 10 minutes. Add zucchini; simmer, covered, further 5 minutes or until vegetables are tender.
3 Make couscous.
4 Stir coriander and juice into vegetables; serve with couscous.
couscous place stock, the water and butter in large saucepan; bring to a boil. Stir in couscous, remove from heat; stand, covered, 3 minutes. Stir with a fork to separate grains.

on the table in 35 minutes
serves 4 **per serving** 24.0g total fat (9.9g saturated fat); 2558kJ (612 cal); 76.9g carbohydrate; 18.1g protein; 7.9g fibre

Rainbow silverbeet with pine nuts, garlic and raisins

750g rainbow silverbeet
2 tablespoons olive oil
1 medium brown onion (150g), chopped
2 cloves garlic, crushed
½ cup (85g) raisins
⅓ cup (50g) pine nuts, toasted
1 tablespoon lemon juice

1 Separate leaves and stems of silverbeet; chop coarsely.
2 Heat half of the oil in large deep frying pan; cook onion and garlic, stirring, until softened. Add silverbeet stems; cook, stirring, until just tender. Add leaves; cook, stirring, until wilted.
3 Remove pan from heat, stir in raisins and half the pine nuts. Drizzle with remaining oil and juice; sprinkle with remaining pine nuts.

on the table in 20 minutes
serves 4 **per serving** 18.5g total fat (1.9g saturated fat); 1162kJ (278 cal); 19.9g carbohydrate; 5.6g protein; 7.5g fibre

Balsamic-glazed baby onions

1 tablespoon balsamic vinegar
1 tablespoon wholegrain mustard
¼ cup (90g) honey
2 tablespoons vegetable oil
500g baby onions, halved

1 Combine vinegar, mustard and honey in small saucepan; bring to a boil. Reduce heat; simmer, uncovered, about 5 minutes or until glaze thickens.
2 Heat oil in large frying pan; cook onions, brushing constantly with glaze, stirring, until browned.

on the table in 25 minutes
serves 8 **per serving** 4.7g total fat (0.6g saturated fat); 372kJ (89 cal); 11.0g carbohydrate; 0.9g protein; 0.6g fibre

Spinach with mint

1 tablespoon vegetable oil
1 large brown onion (200g), sliced thinly
1 teaspoon yellow mustard seeds
¼ teaspoon ground nutmeg
750g trimmed spinach, chopped
1½ tablespoons lemon juice
¼ cup coarsely chopped fresh mint

1 Heat oil in large, deep frying pan; cook onion, stirring, until soft.
2 Add seeds, nutmeg and spinach; cook, stirring until just wilted.
3 Stir through juice and mint.

on the table in 10 minutes
serves 8 **per serving** 2.6g total fat (0.3g saturated fat); 205kJ (49 cal);
2.1g carbohydrate; 2.7g protein; 3.0g fibre
tip yellow mustard seeds are also known as "white", and available from
most supermarkets.

Rag pasta with pumpkin and sage

500g lasagne sheets
¼ cup (60ml) olive oil
50g butter
1kg butternut pumpkin, sliced thinly
2 cloves garlic, sliced thinly
1 teaspoon fresh thyme leaves
½ cup (40g) grated parmesan cheese
2 teaspoons fresh small sage leaves

1 Break lasagne sheets into large pieces. Cook lasagne in large
saucepan of boiling water, uncovered, until just tender. Drain, reserving
2 tablespoons of the cooking liquid.
2 Heat oil and butter in large frying pan; cook pumpkin, stirring gently, until
pumpkin is just tender. Add garlic and thyme; cook, stirring, until fragrant.
3 Add cheese and sage; gently toss through pasta with reserved cooking
liquid. Sprinkle with parmesan flakes, if desired.

on the table in 30 minutes
serves 4 **per serving** 29.4g total fat (11.6g saturated fat); 3189kJ
(763 cal); 101.2g carbohydrate; 22.3g protein; 6.8g fibre

Sautéed potatoes

1kg potatoes, unpeeled
2 tablespoons olive oil
50g butter, chopped

1 Cut potatoes into 1cm-thick slices.
2 Heat oil and butter in large frying pan; cook potato, covered, over medium heat, turning occasionally, until browned lightly. Reduce heat; cook, tossing pan to turn potato slices, about 10 minutes or until tender.

on the table in 25 minutes
serves 4 **per serving** 19.6g total fat (8.0g saturated fat); 1438kJ (344 cal); 33.1g carbohydrate; 6.1g protein; 5.0g fibre

Chickpea and pumpkin curry

In Indian cooking, the word masala loosely translates as paste; the word tikka refers to a bite-sized piece of meat, poultry, fish or vegetable. A jar labelled tikka masala contains spices and oils, mixed into a mild paste.

2 teaspoons peanut oil
2 medium brown onions (300g), sliced thinly
2 cloves garlic, crushed
2 tablespoons tikka masala curry paste
2 cups (500ml) vegetable stock
1 cup (250ml) water
1kg butternut pumpkin, chopped coarsely
2 cups (400g) jasmine rice
300g can chickpeas, rinsed, drained
1 cup (125g) frozen peas
¼ cup (60ml) cream
2 tablespoons coarsely chopped fresh coriander

1 Heat oil in large, deep frying pan; cook onion and garlic, stirring, until onion softens. Add paste; cook, stirring, until fragrant. Stir in stock and the water; bring to a boil. Add pumpkin, reduce heat; simmer, covered, 15 minutes or until pumpkin is almost tender.
2 Cook rice in large saucepan of boiling water, uncovered, until tender; drain. Cover to keep warm.
3 Add chickpeas and peas to curry; cook, stirring, until hot. Stir in cream and coriander. Serve curry with rice.

on the table in 35 minutes
serves 4 **per serving** 15.4g total fat (6.2g saturated fat); 2784kJ (666 cal); 107.2g carbohydrate; 19.3g protein; 9.8g fibre
tip make the curry a day ahead to allow the flavours to develop better.

Mushroom and parsley omelette

4 eggs
6 egg whites
500g swiss brown mushrooms, sliced thinly
⅓ cup coarsely chopped fresh flat-leaf parsley

1 Whisk eggs with egg whites in medium bowl.
2 Cook mushrooms in heated 20cm frying pan, stirring, until tender.
Transfer to small bowl with parsley.
3 Return pan to heat, add a quarter of the egg mixture; cook, tilting pan,
over medium heat until almost set. Place a quarter of the mushroom
mixture evenly over half of the omelette; fold omelette over to enclose
filling, slide onto serving plate. Repeat with remaining egg and mushroom
mixtures to make four omelettes in total.

on the table in 20 minutes
serves 4 **per serving** 5.6g total fat (1.6g saturated fat); 556kJ (133 cal);
2.2g carbohydrate; 16.6g protein; 3.4g fibre

Chats with black mustard seeds and sea salt

1kg tiny new potatoes
2 tablespoons olive oil
1 tablespoon black mustard seeds
2 teaspoons sea salt flakes
1 teaspoon freshly ground black pepper
1 tablespoon coarsely chopped fresh flat-leaf parsley

1 Boil, steam or microwave potatoes until just tender; drain.
2 Heat oil in large frying pan; cook potatoes, stirring, until potatoes are browned lightly. Add mustard seeds, stirring, about 1 minute or until seeds pop.
3 Add remaining ingredients; toss gently to combine.

on the table in 30 minutes
serves 4 **per serving** 9.4g total fat (1.3g saturated fat); 1058kJ (253 cal); 33.0g carbohydrate; 6.0g protein; 5.1g fibre

Fresh peas with caraway and parmesan

You will need about 1.3kg fresh peas in the pod for this recipe.

60g butter
1 teaspoon caraway seeds
2 teaspoons finely grated lemon rind
1 small red onion (100g), sliced thinly
4 cups (600g) shelled fresh peas
⅓ cup coarsely chopped fresh flat-leaf parsley
½ cup (40g) finely grated parmesan cheese

1 Melt butter in large frying pan; cook seeds, rind and onion, stirring, until onion softens.
2 Add peas; cook, stirring, until peas are just tender. Stir in parsley; sprinkle with cheese.

on the table in 35 minutes
serves 8 **per serving** 8.1g total fat (5.1g saturated fat); 598kJ (143 cal); 8.5g carbohydrate; 6.8g protein; 4.8g fibre

Beans and fennel with anchovy dressing

¼ cup (60ml) olive oil
3 baby fennel bulbs (200g), trimmed, quartered
½ cup (125ml) chicken stock
300g baby green beans, trimmed
6 green onions, cut into 8cm lengths
1 teaspoon finely grated lemon rind
6 anchovy fillets, drained, chopped finely
1 clove garlic, crushed
1 teaspoon dijon mustard
2 tablespoons finely chopped fresh flat-leaf parsley

1 Heat 2 teaspoons of the oil in medium frying pan; cook fennel, stirring,
2 minutes. Add stock; simmer, covered, about 5 minutes or until almost
tender. Add beans; simmer, covered, until just tender.
2 Add green onions to pan with rind, anchovies, garlic, mustard and
parsley; stir until warmed through.

on the table in 20 minutes
serves 4 **per serving** 14.3g total fat (2.1g saturated fat); 694kJ (166 cal);
3.8g carbohydrate; 4.2g protein; 3.5g fibre

Little zucchini with crisp crumbs

2 tablespoons olive oil
40g butter
2 thick slices (50g) ciabatta bread, crusts removed, chopped finely
2 cloves garlic, crushed
1 tablespoon pine nuts, toasted, chopped coarsely
1 teaspoon finely grated lemon rind
2 tablespoons finely chopped fresh flat-leaf parsley
1 tablespoon dried currants
24 small zucchini (700g), with flowers attached

1 Heat half of the oil and half of the butter in large frying pan; cook bread cubes, stirring, until browned lightly. Add garlic; cook, stirring, until fragrant. Stir in pine nuts, rind, parsley and currants.
2 Heat remaining oil and butter in large frying pan, add zucchini; cook, covered loosely, until browned lightly and just tender.
3 Serve zucchini sprinkled with the bread mixture.

on the table in 30 minutes
serves 8 **per serving** 10.4g total fat (3.4g saturated fat); 523kJ (125 cal); 5.4g carbohydrate; 2.0g protein; 2.0g fibre
tip crumb mixture can be prepared several hours ahead. Cook zucchini just before serving. If zucchini flowers are not available, substitute small zucchini quartered lengthways.

Mediterranean vegetables with cheese

80g butter
1 medium red capsicum (200g), sliced thinly
1 medium yellow capsicum (200g), sliced thickly
1 medium red onion (170g), cut into wedges
5 small eggplant (330g), chopped coarsely
5 small zucchini (380g), chopped coarsely
150g button mushrooms, halved
¼ cup loosely packed fresh basil leaves
¼ cup (20g) finely grated parmesan cheese
¼ cup (30g) coarsely grated cheddar cheese

1 Heat half of the butter in large frying pan; cook half of the vegetables, stirring, until just tender. Transfer into a 1.5 litre (6 cup) ovenproof dish.
2 Heat remaining butter in same pan; repeat with remaining vegetables.
3 Sprinkle basil and combined cheeses over vegetables in dish. Place under hot grill until cheese melts.

on the table in 35 minutes
serves 4 **per serving** 19.0g total fat (7.1g saturated fat); 1070kJ (256 cal); 9.4g carbohydrate; 9.3g protein; 6.1g fibre

274

Caramelised carrots

1 tablespoon olive oil
30g butter
6 medium carrots (720g), sliced thickly
2 tablespoons white sugar
1 tablespoon finely chopped fresh flat-leaf parsley
1 tablespoon balsamic vinegar

1 Heat oil and butter in large frying pan; cook carrots, covered, over low heat until just tender.
2 Add sugar; cook, stirring constantly, about 10 minutes or until carrots caramelise. Stir in parsley and vinegar.

on the table in 30 minutes
serves 8 **per serving** 5.4g total fat (2.3g saturated fat); 368kJ (88 cal); 8.4g carbohydrate; 0.7g protein; 2.3g fibre
tip this recipe can be made several hours ahead; reheat just before serving.

Cauliflower, pea and fried tofu curry

You will need about 1kg cauliflower for this recipe.

2 tablespoons olive oil
1 medium brown onion (150g), chopped coarsely
2 cloves garlic, crushed
900g cauliflower florets
1 teaspoon ground cumin
½ teaspoon ground coriander
½ teaspoon ground turmeric
¼ teaspoon cayenne pepper
1 teaspoon garam marsala
400g can tomatoes
1 cup (250ml) vegetable stock
¼ cup (60ml) vegetable oil
400g firm tofu, cut into 1cm cubes
1 cup (120g) frozen peas, thawed

1 Heat olive oil in large, deep frying pan; cook onion and garlic, stirring, until onion softens.
2 Add cauliflower and spices; cook, stirring, 2 minutes. Add undrained crushed tomatoes and stock, stir to combine; bring to a boil. Reduce heat; simmer, covered, 10 minutes or until cauliflower softens slightly.
3 Meanwhile, heat vegetable oil in medium frying pan; cook tofu, in batches, until lightly coloured and crisp on all sides. Drain on absorbent paper.
4 Add tofu and peas to cauliflower curry.

on the table in 35 minutes
serves 4 **per serving** 30.8g total fat (4.2g saturated fat); 1797kJ (430 cal); 13.6g carbohydrate; 20.7g protein; 9.5g fibre
tip this recipe is best made close to serving so tofu stays crisp.

Wilted radicchio and fennel

¼ cup (60ml) olive oil
1 clove garlic, crushed
1kg baby fennel bulbs, sliced thinly
1 radicchio (420g), sliced thinly

1 Heat oil in large frying pan; cook garlic and fennel, stirring, until just tender.
2 Add radicchio; stir until almost wilted.

on the table in 15 minutes
serves 6 **per serving** 9.4g total fat (1.3g saturated fat); 481kJ (115 cal); 3.8g carbohydrate; 1.9g protein; 4.2g fibre

Spanish tortilla

Canned tiny new potatoes are a nifty shortcut in this recipe.

1 tablespoon olive oil
1 large brown onion (200g), sliced thinly
750g canned tiny new potatoes, drained, sliced thickly
6 eggs, beaten lightly
100g fetta cheese, chopped coarsely
⅓ cup (25g) finely grated parmesan cheese
⅓ cup (40g) coarsely grated cheddar cheese

1 Heat oil in medium frying pan; cook onion, stirring, until it softens.
2 Combine onion, potato, egg and cheeses in large bowl.
3 Pour potato mixture into heated oiled medium frying pan; cook, covered, over low heat 10 minutes or until egg sets.
4 Carefully invert tortilla onto plate and slide back into frying pan; cook further 5 minutes or until cooked through.
5 Remove from heat; stand 10 minutes before removing from pan.

on the table in 35 minutes
serves 4 **pper serving** 23.9g total fat (10.3g saturated fat); 1668kJ (399 cal); 21.5g carbohydrate; 23.4g protein; 3.2g fibre
tip tortilla can be eaten hot or cold and makes great picnic fare.

boil+
steam

Parmesan mash

1kg potatoes, peeled, cut into 3cm pieces
40g butter, softened
1 cup (80g) grated parmesan cheese
¾ cup (180ml) hot milk, approximately

1 Place potato in medium saucepan with enough cold water to barely
cover the potato. Boil, uncovered, over medium heat about 15 minutes or
until tender. Drain.
2 Using the back of a wooden spoon, push potato through fine sieve
into large bowl. Stir in butter, cheese and enough hot milk, until mash
is smooth and fluffy.
3 Serve topped with a little extra butter, if desired.

on the table in 30 minutes
serves 4 **per serving** 16.7g total fat (10.7g saturated fat); 1442kJ
(345 cal); 32.0g carbohydrate; 14.6g protein; 3.6g fibre

Asparagus and beans with garlic butter

100g butter, softened
2 cloves garlic, crushed
1 tablespoon finely chopped fresh flat-leaf parsley
500g asparagus, trimmed
500g baby green beans

1 Combine butter, garlic and parsley in small bowl; mix well.
2 Boil, steam or microwave asparagus and beans, separately, until just tender; drain.
3 Return asparagus and beans to pan; add butter mixture, toss until melted.

on the table in 15 minutes
serves 8 **per serving** 10.4g total fat (6.8g saturated fat); 489kJ (117 cal); 2.3g carbohydrate; 2.6g protein; 2.5g fibre

Buk choy steamed with chilli oil

4 baby buk choy (600g)
1 tablespoon peanut oil
2 cloves garlic, crushed
2 tablespoons light soy sauce
1½ teaspoons hot chilli sauce
2 green onions, sliced thinly
¼ cup loosely packed fresh coriander leaves
1 fresh small red thai chilli, sliced thinly

1 Halve buk choy lengthways; place, cut-side up, in bamboo steamer. Drizzle buk choy with combined oil, garlic and sauces.
2 Steam buk choy, covered, over wok or large saucepan of simmering water about 5 minutes or until just tender.
3 Serve buk choy sprinkled with onion, coriander and chilli.

on the table in 10 minutes
serves 4 **per serving** 5.1g total fat (0.9g saturated fat); 318kJ (76 cal); 3.7g carbohydrate; 2.5g protein; 2.7g fibre

Lyonnaise potatoes

Lyon is seen as one of the gastronomic capitals of the world, and it's no wonder when the city produces luscious dishes such as this.

900g potatoes, peeled, chopped coarsely
1 tablespoon olive oil
2 medium red onions (340g), sliced thinly
3 cloves garlic, crushed
6 bacon rashers (420g), rind removed, chopped coarsely
¼ cup coarsely chopped fresh mint

1 Boil, steam or microwave potato until just tender; drain.
2 Heat half of the oil in large frying pan; cook onion and garlic, stirring, until onion softens. Remove from pan.
3 Cook bacon in same pan, stirring, until crisp; drain on absorbent paper.
4 Heat remaining oil in same pan, add potato; cook, stirring, 5 minutes or until browned lightly.
5 Return onion mixture and bacon to pan; stir gently to combine with potato. Remove from heat; stir in mint.

on the table in 30 minutes
serves 4 **per serving** 8.0g total fat (1.8g saturated fat); 1191kJ (285 cal); 31.9g carbohydrate; 18.1g protein; 5.0g fibre

293

Leek, zucchini and asparagus with chive butter

1 litre (4 cups) vegetable stock
4 small leeks (400g), halved lengthways
8 small zucchini (360g), halved lengthways
250g asparagus, trimmed
50g butter
1 clove garlic, crushed
¼ cup finely chopped fresh chives

1 Pour stock into large saucepan, bring to a boil; add leeks and zucchini. Reduce heat, simmer gently, uncovered, 3 minutes.
2 Add asparagus; simmer, uncovered, turning occasionally, further 3 minutes or until vegetables are just tender. Drain.
3 Melt butter in same frying pan, add garlic and chives. Return vegetables to pan and toss to coat evenly in butter mixture.

on the table in 20 minutes
serves 6 **per serving** 7.9g total fat (4.8g saturated fat); 456kJ (109 cal); 4.3g carbohydrate; 4.2g protein; 2.7g fibre

Baby beetroot with caper vinaigrette

You will need about 2 bunches of baby beetroot for this recipe.

1kg baby beetroot
1 tablespoon drained baby capers, rinsed
2 tablespoons white wine vinegar
2 tablespoons olive oil
1 teaspoon dijon mustard

1 Remove stems from beetroot; cook beetroot in large saucepan of boiling water, uncovered, about 20 minutes or until tender. Drain; cool 10 minutes. Peel beetroot.
2 Place beetroot in large bowl with remaining ingredients; toss gently to combine.

on the table in 35 minutes
serves 8 **per serving** 4.7g total fat (0.6g saturated fat); 393kJ (94 cal); 9.4g carbohydrate; 2.1g protein; 3.5g fibre

Broccolini and beans with garlic and anchovies

350g broccolini, trimmed
350g baby green beans, trimmed
2 tablespoons olive oil
2 cloves garlic, chopped finely
6 drained anchovies, chopped finely

1 Boil, steam or microwave broccolini and beans, separately, until just tender; drain.
2 Heat oil in large frying pan; cook garlic and anchovies until garlic softens.
3 Add beans and broccolini, toss gently to combine.

on the table in 20 minutes
serves 8 **per serving** 4.9g total fat (0.7g saturated fat); 280kJ (67 cal); 1.3g carbohydrate; 3.2g protein; 2.5g fibre

Mixed peas with mint dressing

You will need about 400g fresh peas in the pod for this recipe.

1 cup (150g) shelled fresh peas
250g sugar snap peas, trimmed
250g snow peas, trimmed
50g snow pea sprouts
100g fetta cheese, crumbled
2 tablespoons toasted pine nuts
¼ cup firmly packed fresh mint leaves
mint dressing
1 teaspoon finely grated lemon rind
2 tablespoons lemon juice
¼ cup (60ml) olive oil
2 tablespoons coarsely chopped fresh mint
1 teaspoon caster sugar

1 Bring a large saucepan of water to a boil; add shelled peas. Boil, uncovered, 1 minute. Add sugar snap peas; boil further 1 minute. Add snow peas; boil 20 seconds or until snow peas change colour. Drain.
2 Place all peas into large bowl of iced water until cold; drain well.
3 Gently toss drained peas with snow pea sprouts in large serving bowl; top with cheese, pine nuts and mint leaves.
4 Make mint dressing; drizzle over peas just before serving.
mint dressing place ingredients in screw-top jar; shake well.

on the table in 30 minutes
serves 6 **per serving** 16.7g total fat (4.1g saturated fat); 936kJ (224 cal); 9.0g carbohydrate; 8.1g protein; 4.0g fibre

Beetroot with garlic sauce

1kg medium beetroot, trimmed
sea salt
garlic sauce
1 medium potato (200g), sliced thickly
4 cloves garlic, chopped coarsely
2 tablespoons cold water
1½ tablespoons lemon juice
½ cup (80ml) olive oil

1 Boil, steam or microwave unpeeled beetroot until tender; drain. Peel while still warm. Cut beetroot into wedges; sprinkle with salt.
2 Make garlic sauce; serve with beetroot.
garlic sauce boil, steam or microwave potato until tender; drain. Mash potato until smooth. Blend or process garlic, water and juice until smooth. While motor is operating, add oil in a thin stream; blend until thick. Stir in potato. (Do not blend or process potato).

on the table in 35 minutes
serves 8 **per serving** 9.3g total fat (1.3g saturated fat); 631kJ (151 cal); 12.5g carbohydrate; 2.7g protein; 4.0g fibre

Steamed spinach

800g baby spinach leaves
¼ cup (60ml) olive oil
2 tablespoons lemon juice

1 Steam or microwave spinach until just wilted; drain well.
2 Transfer spinach to serving dish; pour over combined oil and juice.

on the table in 10 minutes
serves 8 **per serving** 7.1g total fat (1.0g saturated fat); 343kJ (82 cal);
0.7g carbohydrate; 2.4g protein; 2.7g fibre

Fettuccine with cauliflower and broccoli

You will need to buy half a medium cauliflower and about 450g broccoli for this recipe.

125g butter
4 cloves garlic, crushed
½ cup (35g) stale breadcrumbs
2 anchovy fillets, chopped coarsely
4 cups (350g) coarsely chopped cauliflower
4 cups (350g) coarsely chopped broccoli
250g fettuccine pasta

1 Heat butter in large frying pan; cook garlic and breadcrumbs, stirring, until breadcrumbs are golden brown. Stir in anchovy.
2 Bring large saucepan of water to a boil. Add cauliflower and broccoli; cook, stirring to ensure pieces separate. When vegetables are just tender, drain; rinse under cold water, drain.
3 Cook pasta in large saucepan of boiling water, uncovered, until just tender; drain.
4 Place pasta in large bowl with cauliflower, broccoli and breadcrumb mixture; toss gently to combine.

on the table in 30 minutes
serves 4 **per serving** 27.2g total fat (17.1g saturated fat); 2199kJ (526 cal); 51.3g carbohydrate; 15.1g protein; 8.1g fibre

Broccolini polonaise

A "polonaise" – the French interpretation of a classic Polish way of presenting cooked vegetables such as cauliflower, broccoli, asparagus and the like – is a topping of chopped or sieved hard-boiled egg, buttered breadcrumbs and chopped parsley.

60g butter
1 cup (70g) stale breadcrumbs
4 hard-boiled eggs, chopped finely
¼ cup finely chopped fresh flat-leaf parsley
750g broccolini
60g butter, melted

1 Melt butter in large frying pan; cook breadcrumbs, stirring, until browned and crisp.
2 Combine breadcrumbs in small bowl with egg and parsley; mix well.
3 Boil, steam or microwave broccolini until just tender; drain.
4 Top broccolini with polonaise mixture; drizzle with melted butter.

on the table in 20 minutes
serves 8 **per serving** 15.7g total fat (9.0g saturated fat); 882kJ (211 cal); 6.5g carbohydrate; 9.2g protein; 4.3g fibre

Raclette

Like fondue, raclette is a staple winter meal in Switzerland and is traditionally made with the pungent Swiss melting cheese of the same name. You can replace raclette with gruyère, appenzeller or emmental.

4 potatoes (680g), unpeeled
1 cup (125g) coarsely grated raclette cheese
20g butter
1 tablespoon coarsely chopped fresh flat-leaf parsley
½ cup (90g) drained cornichons
½ cup (100g) drained pickled cocktail onions

1 Boil, steam or microwave potatoes until tender; drain.
2 Cut a cross in each potato, taking care not to cut all the way through; gently squeeze potatoes open. Divide cheese among potatoes; top with butter.
3 Place potatoes under hot grill until cheese and butter melt. Sprinkle with parsley; serve with cornichons and onions.

on the table in 30 minutes
serves 4 **per serving** 5.4g total fat (3.4g saturated fat); 489kJ (117 cal); 11.3g carbohydrate; 4.8g protein; 1.6g fibre

Sweet chilli and lime
mixed vegetable salad

200g asparagus, trimmed, chopped coarsely
100g fresh baby corn, sliced lengthways
1 medium red capsicum (200g), sliced thinly
100g shiitake mushrooms, sliced thinly
1 lebanese cucumber (130g), seeded, sliced thinly
12 green onions, sliced thinly
100g bean sprouts
1 fresh small red thai chilli, sliced thinly
2 tablespoons finely chopped fresh coriander
dressing
2 tablespoons lime juice
1 tablespoon sweet chilli sauce
2 teaspoons sesame oil
2 teaspoons fish sauce
1 clove garlic, crushed

1 Boil, steam or microwave asparagus and corn, separately, until just tender; drain. Cool.
2 Combine asparagus and corn in large serving bowl with capsicum, mushroom, cucumber, onion, sprouts, chilli and coriander.
3 Make dressing; drizzle over salad. Toss gently to combine.
dressing place ingredients in screw-top jar; shake well.

on the table in 25 minutes
serves 4 **per serving** 3.1g total fat (0.4g saturated fat); 422kJ (101 cal); 10.3g carbohydrate; 5.3g protein; 4.9g fibre

Green beans and hazelnuts

500g green beans, trimmed
½ cup (60g) hazelnuts, toasted, chopped coarsely
dressing
2 tablespoons red wine vinegar
½ cup (60ml) olive oil
2 teaspoons wholegrain mustard

1 Boil, steam or microwave beans until just tender, drain. Place beans in bowl of iced water until cooled; drain well.
2 Make dressing; gently toss with beans and nuts.
dressing place ingredients in screw top jar; shake well.

on the table in 10 minutes
serves 4 **per serving** 23.2g total fat (2.3g saturated fat); 1053kJ (252 cal); 3.9g carbohydrate; 5.1g protein; 5.0g fibre

Creamed spinach mash

1kg potatoes, chopped coarsely
20g butter
1 clove garlic, crushed
125g baby spinach leaves
300ml cream, warmed

1 Boil, steam or microwave potato until tender; drain.
2 Melt butter in large frying pan; cook garlic and spinach, stirring, until garlic is fragrant and spinach wilted.
3 Blend or process spinach mixture with half of the cream until pureed.
4 Place hot potato in large bowl, mash until smooth; stir in spinach puree and remaining cream.

on the table in 30 minutes
serves 4 **per serving** 36.9g total fat (24.1g saturated fat); 2082kJ (498 cal); 32.1g carbohydrate; 7.7g protein; 4.6g fibre

317

Sesame patty-pan squash and sugar snap peas

16 yellow patty-pan squash (480g)
300g sugar snap peas, trimmed
2 teaspoons sesame oil
1 tablespoon soy sauce
1 tablespoon toasted sesame seeds

1 Boil, steam or microwave squash and peas, separately, until tender; drain.
2 Place vegetables in large bowl with remaining ingredients; toss gently to combine.

on the table in 15 minutes
serves 8 **per serving** 2.2g total fat (0.3g saturated fat); 213kJ (51 cal); 3.6g carbohydrate; 3.0g protein; 2.3g fibre

Fresh asparagus topped with garlic breadcrumbs and chopped eggs

80g butter
2 tablespoons honey
2 cloves garlic, crushed
1 cup (70g) stale breadcrumbs
1kg asparagus, trimmed
2 hard-boiled eggs, chopped finely
⅓ cup coarsely chopped fresh flat-leaf parsley

1 Melt half of the butter and half of the honey in large frying pan. Add garlic and breadcrumbs; cook, stirring, until breadcrumbs are browned and crisp.
2 Boil, steam or microwave asparagus until just tender; drain.
3 Serve asparagus scattered with breadcrumb mixture, egg and parsley; drizzle with combined remaining melted butter and honey.

on the table in 20 minutes
serves 8 **per serving** 9.9g total fat (5.9g saturated fat); 686kJ (164 cal); 13.0g carbohydrate; 5.2g protein; 1.9g fibre
tip this recipe is best made just before serving, so breadcrumbs stay crisp.

Cauliflower with chilli and pine nuts

1 small cauliflower (1kg)
2 tablespoons olive oil
2 cloves garlic, crushed
2 tablespoons pine nuts
2 teaspoons dried chilli flakes
2 tablespoons coarsely chopped fresh flat-leaf parsley

1 Separate cauliflower into pieces. Boil, steam or microwave cauliflower until almost tender; drain, pat dry.
2 Heat oil in medium frying pan; cook garlic, pine nuts and chilli, stirring, over low heat until fragrant and nuts are browned lightly.
3 Add cauliflower; cook, stirring, until well coated with oil mixture.
4 Add parsley; stir until combined.

on the table in 20 minutes
serves 8 **per serving** 7.3g total fat (0.8g saturated fat); 385kJ (92 cal); 2.6g carbohydrate; 3.0g protein; 2.4g fibre

Quartet of beans in chilli lime sauce

270g rice stick noodles
250g frozen broad beans, thawed, peeled
150g green beans, halved
150g snake beans, chopped coarsely
150g butter beans, halved
vegetable oil, for deep-frying
¼ cup (40g) drained capers
1 tablespoon olive oil
6 cloves garlic, crushed
1 small red onion (100g), cut into wedges
4 fresh small red thai chillies, halved lengthways
2 tablespoons finely grated lime rind
1 cup (250ml) vegetable stock

1 Place noodles in medium heatproof bowl; cover with boiling water.
Stand until just tender; drain. Rinse under cold water; drain.
2 Boil, steam or microwave all beans, separately, until just tender; drain.
Heat vegetable oil in small frying pan; deep-fry capers until crisp. Drain
on absorbent paper.
3 Heat olive oil in wok; stir-fry garlic, onion, chilli and rind until onion is soft.
4 Add stock, beans and noodles; cook, stirring gently, until sauce thickens
and mixture is hot.
5 Serve topped with capers.

on the table in 35 minutes
serves 4 **per serving** 6.6g total fat (0.9g saturated fat); 1321kJ (316 cal);
46.9g carbohydrate; 11.1g protein; 10.7g fibre
tip bean thread noodles can be substituted for rice stick noodles.

Buttery mashed celeriac

2kg celeriac, peeled, chopped
90g butter, chopped
1 tablespoon finely chopped fresh chives

1 Boil, steam or microwave celeriac until tender; drain, mash it with most of the butter until smooth.
2 Serve topped with remaining butter and chives.

on the table in 30 minutes
serves 4 **per serving** 19.3g total fat (12.2g saturated fat); 1304kJ (312 cal); 20.2g carbohydrate; 6.6g protein; 17.6g fibre

Beans and sugar snap peas with lemon and capers

300g butter beans
200g sugar snap peas
2 tablespoons drained tiny capers
¼ cup (60ml) lemon juice
2 tablespoons finely chopped fresh dill

1 Boil, steam or microwave beans and sugar snap peas, separately, until just tender; drain.
2 Heat large oiled frying pan; cook capers, stirring, until browned lightly.
3 Add juice, beans and peas to pan; stir until vegetables are hot. Stir in dill.

on the table in 20 minutes
serves 4 **per serving** 0.3g total fat (0.1g saturated fat); 180kJ (43 cal); 4.7g carbohydrate; 3.2g protein; 3.5g fibre

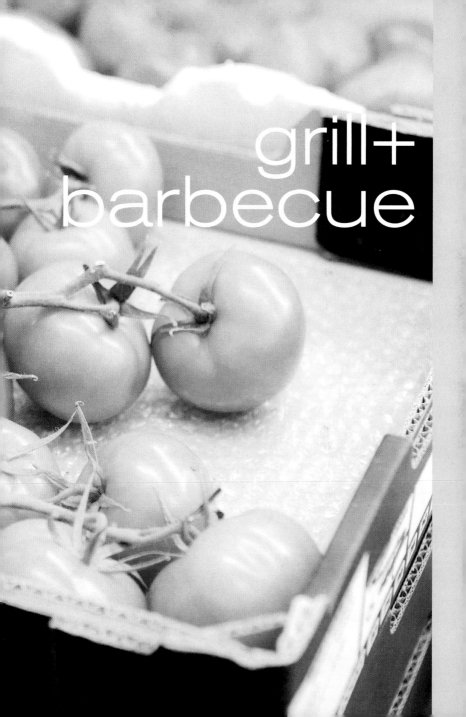

grill+
barbecue

Grilled leeks and green onions with romesco sauce

16 pencil leeks (1.3kg), trimmed
30g butter, melted
1 tablespoon olive oil
300g green onions, trimmed
romesco sauce
1 teaspoon dried chilli flakes
¼ cup (60ml) olive oil
1 large red capsicum (350g), chopped
2 cloves garlic, crushed
1 tablespoon slivered almonds, toasted
2 medium tomatoes (380g), chopped
1 tablespoon red wine vinegar

1 Wash leeks thoroughly to remove grit between leaves.
2 Cook leeks on heated oiled grill plate (or grill or barbecue), brushing with combined butter and oil about 10 minutes or until browned and tender. Add onions; cook until tender.
3 Make romesco sauce.
4 Serve leeks and onions with romesco sauce
romesco sauce soak chilli in 2 tablespoons hot water for 5 minutes; drain. Heat 1 tablespoon of the oil in medium frying pan; cook capsicum and garlic until soft but not coloured. Blend or process chilli with capsicum mixture, almonds and tomatoes until smooth. With motor operating, gradually add remaining oil and vinegar.

on the table in 30 minutes
serves 8 **per serving** 13.7g total fat (3.4g saturated fat); 748kJ (179 cal); 8.1g carbohydrate; 4.1g protein; 5.0g fibre

Grilled stuffed mushrooms

If you can't buy large flat mushrooms, increase the number to give a reasonable-sized serving.

4 medium potatoes (800g), chopped coarsely
1 cup (125g) frozen peas
1 large brown onion (200g), chopped finely
2 cloves garlic, crushed
1 fresh small red thai chilli, chopped finely
2 tablespoons water
4 large flat mushrooms (600g)
2 tablespoons cream
30g butter
½ cup (55g) coarsely grated cheddar cheese
¼ cup coarsely chopped fresh flat-leaf parsley
50g butter, melted, extra

1 Boil, steam or microwave potato and peas, separately, until tender; drain.
2 Combine onion, garlic, chilli and the water in small saucepan; cook, stirring, about 5 minutes or until onion softens.
3 Remove stems from mushrooms.
4 Mash potatoes, peas, cream and butter in large bowl until smooth. Add onion mixture, cheese and parsley; mix well.
5 Brush mushrooms all over with extra butter; cook on heated oiled grill plate (or grill or barbecue) until tender.
6 Divide potato mixture among mushrooms; cook under hot grill about 5 minutes or until potato is lightly browned.

on the table in 35 minutes
serves 4 **per serving** 26.2g total fat (16.6g saturated fat); 1856kJ (444 cal); 31.1g carbohydrate; 16.2g protein; 9.5g fibre
tip it is quicker and easier to fill the mushrooms using a piping bag.

335

Sesame banana chillies, corn and green onions

12 banana chillies (1kg)
350g fresh baby corn
300g green onions, trimmed
2 teaspoons sesame oil
1 teaspoon sesame seeds, toasted

1 Cook chillies on heated oiled grill plate (or griddle or barbecue), until browned on both sides and tender.
2 Add corn and green onions; cook until browned and just tender. Transfer vegetables to serving platter.
3 Drizzle vegetables with sesame oil; sprinkle with seeds before serving.

on the table in 15 minutes
serves 6 **per serving** 2.9g total fat (0.3g saturated fat); 502kJ (120 cal); 15.4g carbohydrate; 4.7g protein; 6.1g fibre

Eggplant, fetta and capsicum stack with mesclun salad

2 medium red capsicums (400g)
¼ cup (60ml) olive oil
2 tablespoons lemon juice
1 clove garlic, crushed
1 large eggplant (500g)
1 cup (150g) drained sun-dried tomatoes, chopped coarsely
¼ cup (50g) seeded kalamata olives, chopped coarsely
½ cup loosely packed fresh basil, torn
100g mesclun
2 tablespoons red wine vinegar
200g fetta cheese, cut into 8 slices
1 tablespoon small fresh basil leaves, extra

1 Quarter capsicums; discard seeds and membranes. Cook capsicum on heated oiled grill plate (or grill or barbecue), skin-side down, until skin blisters and blackens. Cover with plastic wrap for 5 minutes; peel away skin.
2 Combine 2 tablespoons of the oil in small bowl with juice and garlic.
3 Cut eggplant lengthways into 8 slices, brush both sides with oil mixture; cook on heated oiled grill plate, uncovered, brushing occasionally with oil mixture, until just tender.
4 Combine tomato, olives and basil in small bowl. Place mesclun in medium bowl, drizzle with vinegar and remaining oil; toss gently to combine.
5 Place 1 slice of the eggplant on each serving plate; top each with 2 slices of the cheese, 2 pieces of the capsicum and 1 remaining eggplant slice. Top with tomato mixture, sprinkle with extra basil leaves; serve with salad.

on the table in 30 minutes
serves 4 **per serving** 27.8g total fat (9.8g saturated fat); 1797kJ (430 cal); 23.3g carbohydrate; 16.4g protein; 10.2g fibre

Fennel, asparagus, nashi and walnut salad

6 small fennel bulbs (1.2kg), halved lengthways
750g asparagus, trimmed
1 tablespoon olive oil
¼ cup (60ml) walnut oil
2 teaspoons caster sugar
¼ cup (60ml) lemon juice
2 nashi (400g), cored
1 tablespoon finely chopped fresh flat-leaf parsley
½ cup (50g) toasted walnuts, chopped coarsely

1 Cook fennel and asparagus on heated oiled grill plate (or grill or barbecue) brushing with olive oil, until vegetables are just tender.
2 Whisk walnut oil, sugar and juice in large bowl. Cut nashi into thin wedges. Add fennel, nashi, parsley and nuts to dressing; toss gently to combine.
3 Divide asparagus among serving plates; top with salad.

on the table in 30 minutes
serves 4 **per serving** 27.4g total fat (3.2g saturated fat); 1551kJ (371 cal); 20.1g carbohydrate; 7.1g protein; 9.5g fibre

Barbecued corn, broad beans and capsicum

4 trimmed corn cobs (1kg)
500g frozen broad beans, thawed, peeled
1 medium red capsicum (200g), chopped finely
20g butter

1 Cook corn on heated oiled grill plate (or grill or barbecue) until just tender. When cool enough to handle, use a sharp knife to cut kernels from cobs.
2 Boil, steam or microwave broad beans until tender; drain.
3 Place corn and beans in large bowl with remaining ingredients; toss gently to combine.

on the table in 35 minutes
serves 8 **per serving** 3.4g total fat (1.4g saturated fat); 686kJ (164 cal); 21.0g carbohydrate; 7.6g protein; 9.5g fibre

Eggplant, spinach and pumpkin stacks

1 large eggplant (500g)
coarse cooking salt
200g pumpkin, sliced thinly
700g bottled tomato pasta sauce
80g baby spinach leaves
4 green onions, sliced thinly lengthways
1 cup (100g) coarsely grated mozzarella cheese
¼ cup (40g) toasted pine nuts

1 Discard top and bottom of eggplant; cut eggplant lengthways into ten 5mm slices. Discard rounded-skin-side slices. Place remaining eight slices in colander, sprinkle all over with salt; stand 10 minutes.
2 Rinse eggplant well under cold water; pat dry with absorbent paper. Cook eggplant and pumpkin, in batches, on heated oiled grill plate (or grill or barbecue) until tender.
3 Place sauce in medium saucepan; bring to a boil. Reduce heat; simmer, uncovered, 2 minutes.
4 Place four slices of the eggplant, in single layer, on oven tray; top with half of the spinach, half of the pumpkin and half of the onion. Spoon 2 tablespoons of the sauce over each then repeat layering process, using remaining spinach, pumpkin, onion and another 2 tablespoons of the sauce for each stack. Top stacks with remaining eggplant slices; pour over remaining sauce, sprinkle stacks with cheese and nuts. Place under hot grill until cheese browns lightly.

on the table in 30 minutes
serves 4 **per serving** 14.3g total fat (4.2g saturated fat); 1195kJ (286 cal); 23.4g carbohydrate; 13.1g protein; 7.8g fibre
tip weight the eggplant when draining to extract as much water as possible; otherwise, the liquid causes the eggplant to soften and lose its shape when cooked. This process is called disgorging.

Zucchini, eggplant and bean salad

3 medium zucchini (360g)
2 medium eggplant (600g)
4 medium egg tomatoes (600g)
2 x 400g cans cannellini beans, rinsed, drained
½ cup firmly packed fresh coriander leaves
dressing
1 tablespoon cumin seeds
½ cup (125ml) olive oil
⅓ cup (80ml) lemon juice
2 cloves garlic, crushed
1 teaspoon salt
½ teaspoon freshly ground black pepper

1 Cut zucchini lengthways into 5mm slices. Cut eggplant into 5mm rounds.
2 Cook zucchini and eggplant on heated oiled grill plate (or grill or barbecue) until browned on both sides and tender.
3 Cut tomatoes into quarters, remove seeds and chop flesh coarsely.
4 Make dressing.
5 Combine beans, zucchini, eggplant and tomato in large bowl, stir in dressing and coriander.
dressing cook cumin seeds in dry frying pan, stirring, until seeds are fragrant and begin to pop. Place oil, juice, garlic, salt, pepper and cumin seeds in screw-top jar; shake well.

on the table in 25 minutes
serves 6 **per serving** 19.7g total fat (2.8g saturated fat); 974kJ (233 cal); 7.0g carbohydrate; 4.6g protein; 5.8g fibre
tip the small finger eggplants can also be used – slice these lengthways.

Barbecued vegetables and haloumi with lemon basil dressing

150g baby spinach leaves
200g char-grilled red capsicum, sliced thinly
250g grilled artichokes, halved
½ cup (80g) green olives
8 portobello mushrooms (400g)
400g haloumi cheese, sliced thickly
lemon basil dressing
2 tablespoons lemon juice
⅓ cup (80ml) olive oil
1 clove garlic, crushed
2 tablespoons finely shredded fresh basil

1 Combine spinach, capsicum, artichokes and olives in large bowl.
2 Cook mushrooms on an oiled, heated grill plate (or grill or barbecue), loosely covered with foil, about 5 minutes or until browned and tender; cover to keep warm.
3 On same oiled grill plate (or grill or barbecue), cook haloumi quickly and in batches, over high heat until browned lightly on both sides.
4 Make lemon basil dressing.
5 Top spinach mixture with mushrooms, cheese and dressing.
lemon basil dressing place ingredients in screw-top jar; shake well.

on the table in 20 minutes
serves 4 **per serving** 40.9g total fat (14.2g saturated fat); 2224kJ (532 cal); 11.6g carbohydrate; 27.8g protein; 3.9g fibre

Vegetable and tofu skewers

200g swiss brown mushrooms
1 medium green capsicum (200g), chopped coarsely
1 medium red capsicum (200g), chopped coarsely
1 medium yellow capsicum (200g), chopped coarsely
3 baby eggplants (180g), chopped coarsely
350g piece firm tofu, diced into 3cm pieces
8 yellow patty-pan squash (200g), halved
100g baby rocket leaves
blue cheese dressing
50g blue cheese
2 tablespoons buttermilk
200g low-fat yogurt
1 small white onion (80g), grated finely
1 clove garlic, crushed
1 tablespoon finely chopped fresh chives
1 tablespoon lemon juice

1 Thread mushrooms, capsicums, eggplant, tofu and squash, alternately, onto 12 skewers.
2 Cook skewers on heated oiled grill plate (or grill or barbecue) until tofu is browned all over and vegetables are just tender.
3 Make blue cheese dressing.
4 Serve skewers on rocket; drizzle with dressing.
blue cheese dressing crumble cheese into small bowl; stir in remaining ingredients.

on the table in 35 minutes
serves 4 **per serving** 11.1g total fat (3.7g saturated fat); 1091kJ (261 cal); 13.6g carbohydrate; 22.8g protein; 7.0g fibre
tip soak 12 bamboo skewers in cold water for at least an hour to prevent them from splintering and scorching during cooking.

Mushroom and asparagus salad

Swiss brown mushrooms, also known as cremini or roman mushrooms, are similar in appearance to button mushrooms, but are slightly dark brown in colour. The large variety are often called portobello mushrooms.

400g swiss brown mushrooms
200g fresh shiitake mushrooms
500g green asparagus, trimmed
500g white asparagus, trimmed
1 cup loosely packed fresh flat-leaf parsley leaves
2 tablespoons toasted pine nuts
dressing
2 teaspoons finely grated lemon rind
¼ cup (60ml) lemon juice
2 tablespoons olive oil
1 clove garlic, crushed

1 Cook mushrooms and asparagus, in batches, on heated oiled grill plate (or grill or barbecue) until browned and just tender.
2 Make dressing.
3 Combine vegetables in large bowl with parsley, nuts and dressing; toss gently to combine.
dressing place ingredients in screw-top jar; shake well.

on the table in 35 minutes
serves 4 **per serving** 14.9g total fat (1.6g saturated fat); 903kJ (216 cal); 5.5g carbohydrate; 11.1g protein; 7.6g fibre

Grilled radicchio and roasted tomato salad

⅓ cup (80ml) olive oil
1 clove garlic, crushed
6 medium egg tomatoes (450g), halved
4 small radicchio (600g), quartered
2 tablespoons balsamic vinegar
100g baby rocket leaves
⅔ cup (50g) shaved pecorino cheese

1 Preheat oven to 220°C/200°C fan-forced.
2 Combine 1 tablespoon of the oil with garlic in small bowl. Place tomato, cut-side up, on oven tray; drizzle with oil mixture. Roast, uncovered, in oven about 20 minutes or until softened.
3 Combine radicchio with 2 tablespoons of the remaining oil in large bowl. Cook radicchio on heated oiled grill plate (or grill or barbecue) until browned all over; cool 5 minutes.
4 Place vinegar and remaining oil in screw-top jar; shake well. Arrange tomato, radicchio and rocket on large serving platter; sprinkle with cheese, drizzle with dressing.

on the table in 30 minutes
serves 6 **per serving** 14.9g total fat (3.2g saturated fat); 681kJ (163 cal); 2.9g carbohydrate; 4.6g protein; 3g fibre

Pumpkin and haloumi salad

650g pumpkin, cut into thin wedges
200g green beans, halved
2 tablespoons olive oil
2 tablespoons red wine vinegar
¾ cup loosely packed fresh coriander leaves
¾ cup loosely packed fresh flat-leaf parsley leaves
100g baby spinach leaves
⅓ cup (55g) toasted pepitas
250g haloumi cheese, sliced thickly

1 Boil, steam or microwave pumpkin and beans, separately, until almost tender; drain. Rinse under cold water; drain. Cook pumpkin on heated oiled grill plate (or grill or barbecue) until browned and tender.
2 Place oil, vinegar, coriander, parsley, spinach and pepitas in large bowl; toss gently to combine.
3 Cook haloumi on same heated oiled grill plate (or grill or barbecue) until browned both sides. Add cheese, pumpkin and beans to bowl with spinach mix; toss gently to combine.

on the table in 25 minutes
serves 4 **per serving** 7.7g total fat (2.6g saturated fat); 497kJ (119 cal); 3.5g carbohydrate; 5.6g protein; 1.8g fibre

Fresh corn and zucchini chunky salsa

2 corn cobs (800g), trimmed
100g baby zucchini, halved lengthways
2 large avocados (640g), chopped coarsely
200g grape tomatoes, halved
1 medium red onion (170g), halved, sliced thickly
¼ cup coarsely chopped fresh coriander
dressing
1 tablespoon sweet chilli sauce
⅓ cup (80ml) lime juice
2 fresh small red thai chillies, sliced thinly

1 Cook corn and zucchini on heated oiled grill plate (or grill or barbecue) until browned lightly and tender. When corn is cool enough to handle, use a sharp knife to cut kernels from cobs.
2 Combine corn and zucchini in large serving bowl with avocado, tomato, onion and coriander.
3 Make dressing; drizzle over salsa. Toss gently to combine.
dressing place ingredients in screw-top jar; shake well.

on the table in 20 minutes
serves 4 **per serving** 27.4g total fat (5.7g saturated fat); 1777kJ (425 cal); 29.5g carbohydrate; 9.7g protein; 10.4g fibre
tip you can substitute cherry tomatoes if you cannot find the grape variety.

Vegetable kebabs with balsamic dressing

250g cherry tomatoes
1 large green capsicum (350g), chopped coarsely
6 small flat mushrooms (600g), quartered
6 yellow patty-pan squash (240g), halved
3 baby eggplant (180g), sliced thickly
3 small zucchini (270g), sliced thickly
1 medium brown onion (150g), sliced thickly
500g haloumi cheese, cubed
60g baby rocket leaves
balsamic dressing
⅓ cup (80ml) olive oil
¼ cup (60ml) balsamic vinegar
1 teaspoon caster sugar

1 Thread tomatoes, vegetables and cheese onto 12 skewers.
2 Cook kebabs, in batches, on heated oiled grill plate (or grill or barbecue) until browned on all sides.
3 Make balsamic dressing.
4 Serve kebabs on rocket leaves drizzled with balsamic dressing.
balsamic dressing place ingredients in screw-top jar; shake well.

on the table in 35 minutes
serves 4 **per serving** 40.8g total fat (16.3g saturated fat); 2470kJ (591 cal); 15.1g carbohydrate; 37.2g protein; 9.6g fibre
tip soak 12 bamboo skewers in cold water for at least an hour to prevent them from splintering and scorching during cooking.

Grilled vegetable salad

2 medium green capsicums (400g)
2 medium red capsicums (400g)
2 medium yellow capsicums (400g)
1 large red onion (300g)
2 medium green zucchini (240g)
2 medium yellow zucchini (240g)
6 baby eggplants (360g)
1 tablespoon fresh oregano leaves
balsamic dressing
2 tablespoons lemon juice
1 clove garlic, crushed
¼ cup (60ml) olive oil
2 tablespoons balsamic vinegar

1 Quarter capsicums, remove and discard seeds and membranes. Cut into thick strips. Cut onion into 8 wedges.
2 Slice zucchini and eggplants lengthways into thin slices.
3 Cook vegetables, in batches, on heated oiled grill plate (or grill or barbecue) until browned all over and tender.
4 Make balsamic dressing.
5 Place vegetables and oregano in large bowl with dressing; toss gently to combine.
balsamic dressing place ingredients in screw-top jar; shake well.

on the table in 35 minutes
serves 6 **per serving** 9.8g total fat (1.3g saturated fat); 673kJ (161 cal); 10.3g carbohydrate; 5.3g protein; 5.0g fibre
tip make this salad the day before you intend to serve it, to infuse the grilled vegetables with the flavour of the dressing.

Barbecued kipflers

12 kipfler potatoes (1.5kg), unpeeled
2 tablespoons coarsely chopped fresh oregano
¼ cup loosely packed fresh thyme leaves
1 tablespoon coarsely grated lemon rind
2 cloves garlic, crushed
⅓ cup (80ml) olive oil
¼ cup (60ml) lemon juice

1 Boil, steam or microwave potatoes until tender; drain. Halve potatoes lengthways.
2 Combine herbs, rind, garlic and oil in large bowl, add potato; toss potato to coat in mixture. Cook potato on heated oiled grill plate (or grill or barbecue) until browned and tender.
3 Serve potato drizzled with juice.

on the table in 35 minutes
serves 8 **per serving** 9.3g total fat (1.3g saturated fat); 890kJ (213 cal); 25.1g carbohydrate; 4.6g protein; 3.4g fibre

Mushroom, tomato and zucchini skewers with white bean puree

1 large red onion (300g), cut into wedges
200g button mushrooms
250g cherry tomatoes
2 large zucchini (300g), chopped coarsely
2 tablespoons balsamic vinegar
2 tablespoons olive oil
white bean puree
2 x 400g cans white beans, rinsed, drained
1 cup (250ml) chicken stock
1 clove garlic, quartered
1 tablespoon lemon juice
1 tablespoon olive oil

1 Make white bean puree.
2 Thread onion, mushrooms, tomatoes and zucchini equally among 12 skewers. Place skewers on large oven tray; drizzle with combined vinegar and oil.
3 Cook skewers on heated oiled grill plate (or grill or barbecue) until browned all over and tender.
4 Serve skewers with white bean puree.
white bean puree place beans and stock in large saucepan; bring to a boil. Reduce heat, simmer, uncovered, about 10 minutes or until liquid is absorbed. Blend or process bean mixture with garlic, juice and oil until smooth.

on the table in 30 minutes
serves 4 **per serving** 14.7g total fat (2.2g saturated fat); 932kJ (223 cal); 11.2g carbohydrate; 8.0g protein; 7.3g fibre
tips soak 12 bamboo skewers in cold water for at least an hour to prevent them from splintering and scorching during cooking.
Many varieties of already cooked white beans are available canned, among them cannellini, butter and haricot beans; any of these are suitable for this puree.

roasts

Roasted vegetable and balsamic salad

Lamb's lettuce, also known as mâche or corn salad, has a mild, almost nutty flavour and dark green leaves. It is usually sold in 125g punnets, but the leaves probably weigh only about a quarter of that total.

¼ cup (60ml) olive oil
1 clove garlic, crushed
2 large green zucchini (300g)
4 medium flat mushrooms (500g), quartered
4 large egg tomatoes (360g), quartered
1 medium red onion (170g), cut into wedges
150g lamb's lettuce (mâche), trimmed
⅓ cup coarsely chopped fresh basil
dressing
¼ cup (60ml) olive oil
2 tablespoons balsamic vinegar
½ teaspoon caster sugar
½ teaspoon dijon mustard
1 clove garlic, crushed

1 Preheat oven to 220°C/200°C fan-forced.
2 Combine oil and garlic in small bowl. Halve zucchini lengthways then chop into thin wedge-shaped pieces on the diagonal.
3 Arrange vegetable pieces, in single layer, on oven trays, brush with oil and garlic mixture; roast, uncovered, about 20 minutes or until browned lightly and just tender. Remove from oven; cool 10 minutes.
4 Make dressing.
5 Place vegetables in large bowl with lettuce, basil and dressing; toss gently to combine.
dressing place ingredients in screw-top jar; shake well.

on the table in 35 minutes
serves 4 **per serving** 28.1g total fat (3.9g saturated fat); 1367kJ (327 cal); 8.0g carbohydrate; 7.4g protein; 7.0g fibre

Couscous-stuffed capsicums

4 large red capsicums (1.4kg)
1½ cups (300g) couscous
1½ cups (375ml) boiling water
½ cup (75g) shelled pistachios
½ cup (70g) slivered almonds, toasted
½ cup (75g) dried currants
¾ cup (180ml) vegetable stock
1 cup (200g) rinsed, drained, canned chickpeas
2 tablespoons coarsely chopped fresh coriander
¾ cup (210g) yogurt
1 lebanese cucumber (130g), grated coarsely

1 Cut off and reserve capsicum tops; remove and discard seeds and membranes. Place capsicums in large microwave-safe dish; cook, covered, on high (100%) for 2 minutes. Cool.
2 Preheat oven to 200°C/180°C fan-forced.
3 Combine couscous and the water in large heatproof bowl, cover; stand 5 minutes or until water is absorbed, fluffing with fork occasionally. Add nuts, currants, stock, chickpeas and coriander; mix well.
4 Divide couscous mixture among capsicums, cover each with reserved capsicum top. Place capsicums in oiled ovenproof dish; roast, uncovered, 20 minutes.
5 Meanwhile, combine yogurt and cucumber in small bowl. Serve stuffed capsicums with yogurt mixture.

on the table in 35 minutes
serves 4 **per serving** 23.3g total fat (3.2g saturated fat); 3043kJ (728 cal); 95.4g carbohydrate; 28.4g protein; 11.2g fibre
tips you can prepare the couscous filling a day ahead. Cover, refrigerate until required.
You could use tomato, eggplant or zucchini shells instead of capsicum.

Roast pumpkin and goat cheese salad

1kg pumpkin, chopped finely
2 tablespoons olive oil
2 cloves garlic, sliced thinly
2 tablespoons finely chopped fresh sage
½ cup (70g) pecans, chopped coarsely
8 large radicchio leaves (120g)
200g goat cheese
2 tablespoons lemon juice

1 Preheat oven to 220°C/200°C fan-forced.
2 Combine pumpkin and half of the oil on oven tray; roast, uncovered, 10 minutes. Add garlic and sage; roast, uncovered, about 5 minutes or until pumpkin is tender. Stir in nuts.
3 Divide radicchio leaves among serving plates; divide pumpkin mixture among leaves, top with cheese. Drizzle with combined juice and remaining oil; top with fresh sage leaves, if desired.

on the table in 30 minutes
serves 4 **per serving** 30.5g total fat (7.9g saturated fat); 1609kJ (385 cal); 15.2g carbohydrate; 13.1g protein; 4.7g fibre

Roasted tomato salad

250g tear-drop tomatoes, halved
250g cherry tomatoes, halved
1 tablespoon olive oil
⅓ cup coarsely chopped fresh flat-leaf parsley
1 fresh small red thai chilli, sliced thinly
2 tablespoons balsamic vinegar
⅓ cup (80ml) olive oil, extra

1 Preheat oven to 220°C/200°C fan-forced.
2 Combine tomatoes, oil, parsley and chilli in small baking dish. Roast, uncovered, about 5 minutes or until just soft.
3 Serve tomatoes, warm or cooled, drizzled with combined vinegar and extra oil.

on the table in 15 minutes
serves 4 **per serving** 22.9g total fat (3.2g saturated fat); 932kJ (223 cal); 2.8g carbohydrate; 0.7g protein; 2.2g fibre

Italian-style stuffed mushrooms

Marsala is a sweet fortified wine originally from Sicily; it can be found
in liquor stores.

8 medium flat mushrooms (800g)
90g butter
½ medium red capsicum (100g), chopped finely
1 clove garlic, crushed
¼ cup (60ml) marsala
1 tablespoon lemon juice
1½ cups (110g) stale breadcrumbs
2 tablespoons coarsely chopped fresh flat-leaf parsley
1 cup (80g) coarsely grated pecorino cheese

1 Preheat oven to 200°C/180°C fan-forced.
2 Carefully remove stems from mushrooms; chop stems finely.
3 Melt butter in small frying pan. Brush mushroom caps with about half
of the butter; place on oiled oven trays.
4 Cook capsicum and garlic, stirring, in remaining butter until capsicum
is just tender. Add chopped mushroom stems, marsala, juice and
breadcrumbs; cook, stirring, 3 minutes. Remove from heat; stir in parsley
and cheese.
5 Spoon filling into mushroom caps; roast, uncovered, about 10 minutes
or until browned lightly.

on the table in 30 minutes
serves 4 **per serving** 25.5g total fat (15.8g saturated fat); 1705kJ
(408 cal); 22.6g carbohydrate; 17.1g protein; 6.5g fibre
tip vegetable stock can be substituted for marsala, if desired.

Roasted pumpkin, sesame and rocket salad

You will need a piece of pumpkin weighing about 750g for this recipe; we used butternut, but you can use whatever pumpkin variety you like.

600g trimmed pumpkin
cooking-oil spray
1 tablespoon honey
1 tablespoon sesame seeds
500g asparagus, trimmed, halved
150g baby rocket leaves
1 small red onion (100g), sliced thinly
1 tablespoon sesame oil
1 tablespoon cider vinegar
1 teaspoon honey, extra

1 Preheat oven to 240°C/220°C fan-forced. Line baking dish with baking paper.
2 Cut pumpkin into 1.5cm wide strips.
3 Place pumpkin, in single layer, in baking dish; spray lightly with cooking-oil spray. Roast, uncovered, about 20 minutes or until pumpkin is just tender. Drizzle with honey; sprinkle with seeds. Roast, uncovered, about 5 minutes, or until seeds are browned lightly.
4 Boil, steam or microwave asparagus until just tender; drain. Rinse under cold water; drain.
5 Combine pumpkin, asparagus, rocket and onion in large bowl. Drizzle with combined remaining ingredients; toss gently.

on the table in 35 minutes
serves 6 **per serving** 5.1g total fat (0.8g saturated fat); 493kJ (118 cal); 12.4g carbohydrate; 4.5g protein; 2.6g fibre
tip reserve any seeds or honey from pumpkin pan and add to dressing.

Roasted truss tomatoes with crispy basil leaves

500g baby vine-ripened truss tomatoes
2 cloves garlic, sliced thinly
1 tablespoon olive oil
2 teaspoons balsamic vinegar
vegetable oil, for deep-frying
⅓ cup loosely packed fresh basil leaves

1 Preheat oven to 180°C/160°C fan-forced.
2 Place tomatoes on oven tray; pour combined garlic, oil and vinegar over tomatoes. Roast, uncovered, about 10 minutes or until tomatoes soften.
3 Heat vegetable oil in small saucepan; deep-fry basil leaves, in batches, until crisp.
4 Serve tomatoes sprinkled with deep-fried basil.

on the table in 20 minutes
serves 8 **per serving** 2.5g total fat (0.3g saturated fat); 134kJ (32 cal); 1.5g carbohydrate; 0.4g protein; 1.2g fibre

Mixed garlic mushrooms

250g flat mushrooms
2 tablespoons olive oil
250g swiss brown mushrooms
250g button mushrooms
1 clove garlic, sliced thinly
¼ cup loosely packed fresh flat-leaf parsley leaves

1 Preheat oven to 200°C/180°C fan-forced.
2 Place flat mushrooms in large baking dish, drizzle with half of the oil.
Roast, uncovered, 10 minutes.
3 Add remaining mushrooms, oil and garlic; roast further 15 minutes or
until mushrooms are tender and browned lightly. Stir in parsley.

on the table in 30 minutes
serves 4 **per serving** 9.7g total fat (1.3g saturated fat); 564kJ (135 cal);
2.9g carbohydrate; 6.9g protein; 5.0g fibre

Spicy roasted pumpkin couscous

1 tablespoon olive oil
2 cloves garlic, crushed
1 large red onion (200g), sliced thickly
500g pumpkin, peeled, chopped coarsely
3 teaspoons ground cumin
2 teaspoons ground coriander
1 cup (200g) couscous
1 cup (250ml) boiling water
20g butter
2 tablespoons coarsely chopped fresh flat-leaf parsley

1 Preheat oven to 220°C/200°C fan-forced.
2 Heat oil in medium flameproof baking dish; cook garlic, onion and pumpkin, stirring, until vegetables are browned lightly. Add spices; cook, stirring, about 2 minutes or until fragrant.
3 Roast, uncovered, about 15 minutes or until pumpkin is just tender.
4 Meanwhile, combine couscous with the water and butter in large heatproof bowl; cover, stand about 5 minutes or until water is absorbed, fluffing with fork occasionally to separate the grains.
5 Add pumpkin mixture to couscous; stir in parsley.

on the table in 30 minutes
serves 4 **per serving** 9.5g total fat (3.7g saturated fat); 1338kJ (320 cal); 47.8g carbohydrate; 9.4g protein; 2.7g fibre

glossary

almonds

meal also known as ground almonds; nuts are powdered to a coarse flour texture.

blanched brown skins removed.

slivered small pieces cut lengthways.

bacon rashers also known as bacon slices; made from cured and smoked pork side.

baking powder a raising agent consisting mainly of two parts cream of tartar to one part bicarbonate of soda.

basil

opal has large purple leaves and a sweet, almost gingery flavour. Can replace thai basil but not holy basil in recipes.

sweet the most common type of basil; used extensively in Italian dishes and one of the main ingredients in pesto.

bean sprouts also known as bean shoots.

beetroot also known as red beets; firm, round root vegetable.

besan flour also known as chickpea flour; made from chickpeas. Available from health food stores.

bicarbonate of soda also called baking soda.

black bean sauce an Asian cooking sauce made from salted fermented soybeans, spices and wheat flour; used mostly in stir-fries.

buk choy also known as bok choy, pak choi, chinese white cabbage or chinese chard; has a fresh, mild mustard taste. Use stems and leaves, stir-fried or braised.

breadcrumbs, stale crumbs made by grating, blending or processing 1- or 2-day-old bread.

broccolini a cross between broccoli and chinese kale; long asparagus-like stems with a long loose floret, both completely edible. Resembles broccoli in looks, but is milder and sweeter in taste.

burghul also known as bulghur wheat; hulled steamed wheat kernels that, once dried, are crushed into various size grains. Different to cracked wheat.

butter we use salted butter unless stated otherwise; 125g is equal to 1 stick (4oz). Unsalted or "sweet" butter has no salt added.

butter beans also known as lima beans; large, flat, kidney-shaped bean, off-white in colour, with a mealy texture and mild taste. Available canned and dried.

buttermilk in spite of its name, it's actually low in fat, varying between 0.6 per cent and 2.0 per cent per 100ml. Available from the dairy department in supermarkets.

capers the grey-green buds of a warm climate (usually Mediterranean) shrub, sold either dried and salted or pickled in a vinegar brine; baby capers are also available both in brine or dried in salt.

capsicum also known as pepper or bell pepper.

celeriac tuberous root with knobbly brown skin, white flesh and a celery-like flavour.

cheese

blue mould-treated cheese mottled with blue veining. Varieties include firm and crumbly stilton types and mild, creamy brie-like types.

bocconcini meaning 'mouthful' in Italian; walnut-sized, baby mozzarella, a delicate, semi-soft, white cheese traditionally made from buffalo milk. Sold fresh, it spoils rapidly so will only keep, refrigerated in brine, for 1 or 2 days at the most.

cheddar the most common cow-milk tasty cheese; should be aged, hard and have a pronounced bite. For a low-fat version, we use one with no more than 20 per cent fat.

fetta Greek in origin; a crumbly textured goat- or sheep-milk cheese with a sharp, salty taste. Ripened and stored in salted whey; particularly good cubed and tossed into salads. We use a version having no more than 15 per cent fat when calling for low-fat cheese.

goat made from goat milk, has an earthy, strong taste. Available in soft, crumbly and firm textures, in various shapes and sizes, and sometimes rolled in ash or herbs.

haloumi a Greek Cypriot cheese with a semi-firm, spongy texture and very salty yet sweet flavour. Ripened and stored in salted whey; it's best grilled or fried, and holds its shape well on being heated. Should be eaten while still warm as it becomes tough and rubbery on cooling.

parmesan also known as parmigiano; is a hard, grainy cow-milk cheese originating in the Parma region of Italy. The curd is salted in brine for a month, then aged for up to 2 years. Grated or flaked, it's used for pasta, salads and soups; is also eaten on its own with fruit. Reggiano is the best, aged for a minimum

2 years and made only in the Italian region of Emilia-Romagna.

pecorino the Italian generic name for sheep-milk cheeses; are classified according to the region they were produced in – romano (Rome), sardo (Sardinia), siciliano (Sicily) and toscano (Tuscany). If not available, use parmesan.

raclette a Swiss cow-milk cheese with a hard, rosy-brown rind and semi-soft interior dotted with small holes. Used in Switzerland and Alsace to make a dish of the same name: cheese is melted on a special raclette grill and poured over steamed or boiled baby potatoes. Heating releases its unique fruity and nutty flavour and intensifies its aroma. It can be used to replace gruyére in a recipe.

ricotta a soft, sweet, moist, white cow-milk cheese with a low fat content (about 8.5 per cent) and a slightly grainy texture. The name roughly means "cooked again" and refers to ricotta's manufacture from a whey that is itself a by-product of other cheese making.

chickpeas also known as garbanzos, hummus or channa; an irregularly round, sandy-coloured legume.

chilli always use rubber gloves when seeding and chopping fresh chillies as they can burn your skin. We use unseeded chillies in our recipes as the seeds contain the heat; use fewer chillies rather than seeding the lot.

banana a sweet flavoured chilli with a long, tapering shape. If unavailable, substitute with red capsicum.

cayenne also known as cayenne pepper; a thin-fleshed, long, extremely hot, dried red chilli, usually purchased ground.

dried flakes also sold as crushed chilli; dehydrated deep-red extremely fine slices and whole seeds; good in cooking or sprinkled over a dish as a seasoning.

powder the Asian variety is the hottest, made from dried ground thai chillies; can be used instead of fresh chillies in the proportion of ½ teaspoon chilli powder to 1 medium chopped fresh red chilli.

sweet chilli sauce a comparatively mild, sticky and runny bottled sauce made from red chillies, sugar, garlic and white vinegar; used in Thai cooking and as a condiment.

thai also known as "scuds"; tiny, very hot and bright red in colour.

choy sum also known as pakaukeo or flowering cabbage, a member of the buk choy family; easy to identify with its long stems, light green leaves and yellow flowers. Stems and leaves are both edible.

coconut cream obtained commercially from the first pressing of coconut flesh alone, without the addition of water; the second pressing (less rich) is sold as coconut milk. Available in cans and cartons at most supermarkets.

coriander also known as cilantro or chinese parsley; bright-green-leafed herb with a pungent aroma and taste.

cornflour also called cornstarch.

cornichons French for gherkin, a very small variety of cucumber.

couscous a fine, grain-like cereal product made from semolina; popular in North African countries. It is eaten like rice with a tagine, as a side dish or salad ingredient.

ginger also known as green or root ginger; the thick gnarled root of a tropical plant. Store, peeled, covered with dry sherry in a jar and refrigerated, or frozen in an airtight container.

hoisin sauce a thick, sweet and spicy chinese barbecue sauce made from salted fermented soybeans, onions and garlic; used as a marinade or baste, or to accent stir-fries and barbecued or roasted foods. From Asian food shops and supermarkets.

kaffir lime leaves also known as bai magrood; look like they are two glossy dark green leaves joined end to end, forming a rounded hourglass shape. Used fresh or dried in many South East Asian dishes, they are used like bay leaves or curry leaves, especially in Thai cooking. Sold fresh, dried or frozen, dried leaves are less potent so double the number if using them as a substitute for fresh; a strip of fresh lime peel may be substituted for each kaffir lime leaf.

kang kong also called chinese water spinach and swamp spinach. Both the long pointed leaves and hollow stems are used like spinach in soups and stir-fries.

kecap manis a dark, thick sweet soy sauce used in most South East Asian cuisines. Is sweetened with the addition of either palm sugar or molasses when brewed. Use as a condiment, dipping sauce, ingredient or marinade.

kumara the polynesian name of an orange-fleshed sweet potato often confused with yam; good baked, boiled, mashed or fried similarly to other potatoes.

lebanese cucumber short, slender and thin-skinned. Probably the most popular variety because of its tender, edible skin, tiny, yielding seeds, and sweet, fresh and flavoursome taste.

lemon grass tall, clumping, lemon-smelling and tasting, sharp-edged aromatic tropical grass; the white lower part of the stem is used, finely chopped, in much of the cooking of South East Asia. Can be found, fresh, dried, powdered and frozen, in supermarkets and greengrocers as well as Asian food shops.

mayonnaise we use whole-egg mayonnaise.

mesclun pronounced mess-kluhn; also known as mixed greens or spring salad mix. A commercial blend of assorted young lettuce and other green leaves, including baby spinach leaves, mizuna and curly endive.

mint, vietnamese not a mint at all, but a pungent and peppery narrow-leafed member of the buckwheat family. Not confined to

Vietnam, it is also known as cambodian mint, pak pai (Thailand), laksa leaf (Indonesia), daun kesom (Singapore) and rau ram in Vietnam. Is common in Thai foods like soups, salads and stir-fries.

mirin a Japanese champagne-coloured cooking wine, made of glutinous rice and alcohol used expressly for cooking; not to be confused with sake.

mizuna Japanese in origin; the frizzy green salad leaves have a delicate mustard flavour.

noodles

crunchy crispy egg noodles, deep-fried then packaged.

dried rice also known as rice stick noodles. Made from rice flour and water, available flat and wide or very thin (vermicelli). Must be soaked in boiling water to soften.

rice stick also known assen lek, ho fun or kway teow; especially popular South East Asian dried rice noodles. They come in different widths (thin used in soups, wide in stir-fries), but all should be soaked in hot water to soften. Is the traditional noodle used in pad thai which, before soaking, measures about 5mm in width.

rice vermicelli also known as sen mee, mei fun or bee hoon. Used throughout Asia in spring rolls and cold salads; similar to bean threads, only longer and made with rice flour instead of mung bean starch. Before using, soak dried noodles in hot water until softened, boil briefly then rinse with hot water. Can also be deep-fried until crunchy, then used in salads, or as a garnish or bed for sauces.

oil

cooking oil spray we use a cholesterol-free canola oil spray.

macadamia made from crushed macadamias.

olive made from ripened olives. Extra virgin and virgin are the first and second press, respectively, of the olives and are therefore considered the best; the "extra light" or "light" name on other types refers to taste not fat levels.

peanut pressed from ground peanuts; the most commonly used oil in Asian cooking due to its high smoking point (capacity to handle high heat without burning).

sesame made from roasted, crushed, white sesame seeds; used as a flavouring rather than a cooking medium.

vegetable any of a number of oils sourced from plant rather than animal fats.

walnut pressed from ground walnuts.

onion

green also called scallion or (incorrectly) shallot; an immature onion picked before the bulb has formed, having a long, bright-green edible stalk.

red also known as spanish, red spanish or bermuda onion; a sweet-flavoured, large, purple-red onion.

shallots also called french shallots, golden shallots or eschalots. Small, elongated and brown-skinned, they grow in tight clusters similar to garlic.

purple shallots also known as Asian shallots; related to the onion but resembling garlic (they grow in bulbs of multiple cloves). Thin-layered and intensely flavoured, they are used throughout South East Asia.

spring crisp, narrow green-leafed tops and a round sweet white bulb larger than green onions.

orange flower water concentrated flavouring made from orange blossoms.

oyster sauce Asian in origin, this thick, richly flavoured brown sauce is made from oysters and their brine, cooked with salt and soy sauce, and thickened.

pak choy also known as tat soi, rosette and chinese flat cabbage; a member of the same family as buk choy, it has the same mild flavour. Its dark-green leaves are usually eaten in salads, but are also good in soups, curries and stir-fries.

pancetta an Italian unsmoked bacon, pork belly cured in salt and spices then rolled into a sausage shape and dried for several weeks.

pepitas pale green kernels of dried pumpkin seeds; plain or salted.

pine nuts also known as pignoli; not in fact a nut but a small, cream-coloured kernel from pine cones. They are best roasted before use to bring out the flavour.

plum sauce a thick, sweet and sour dipping sauce made from plums, vinegar, sugar, chillies and spices.

raisins dried sweet grapes (traditionally muscatel grapes).

rice
basmati white, fragrant long-grained rice; grains fluff up beautifully when cooked. Wash several times before cooking.

jasmine also known as Thai jasmine, is a long-grained white rice with a perfumed aromatic quality; moist in texture, it clings together after cooking. Often used instead of basmati rice.

rice paper sheets there are two products sold as rice paper. Banh trang is made from rice flour and water then stamped into rounds; is brittle and breaks easily. Dipped briefly in water, they become pliable wrappers for food. The other, edible, translucent glossy rice paper is a dough made of water combined with the pith of an Asian shrub called the rice-paper plant (or rice-paper tree). Resembling a grainy sheet of paper and whiter than banh trang, it is imported from Holland. Use in confectionery making and baking; never eat it uncooked.

rigani also known as greek oregano; a stronger, sharper version of the familiar herb used in Italian cooking.

rocket also known as arugula, rugula and rucola; peppery green leaf eaten raw in salads or used in cooking. Baby rocket leaves are smaller and less peppery.

saffron stigma of a member of the crocus family; imparts a yellow-orange colour once infused. Available ground or in strands, the quality can vary greatly; the best is the most expensive spice in the world.

sambal oelek also ulek or olek; Indonesian in origin, this is a salty paste made from ground chillies and vinegar.

savoy cabbage large, heavy head with crinkled dark-green outer leaves and a fairly mild taste.

silverbeet also known as swiss chard and (incorrectly) spinach; has fleshy stalks and large leaves.

snow peas also called mangetout; a variety of garden pea, eaten pod and all. Used in stir-fries or eaten raw in salads. Snow pea sprouts are also available from supermarkets or greengrocers and are usually eaten raw in salads or sandwiches.

soy sauce also known as sieu, is made from fermented soy beans. Several variations are available in most supermarkets and Asian food stores. We used a mild Japanese variety.

spinach also known as english spinach and (incorrectly) silverbeet.

sugar snap peas also known as honey snap peas; fresh small pea which can be eaten whole, pod and all.

sugar

brown an extremely soft, fine granulated sugar retaining molasses for its characteristic colour and flavour.

caster also known as superfine or finely granulated table sugar. The fine crystals dissolve easily so it is perfect for cakes, meringues and desserts.

palm also known as nam tan pip, jaggery, jawa or gula melaka; made from the sap of the sugar palm tree. Light brown to black in colour and usually sold in rock-hard cakes; substitute with brown sugar if unavailable.

white we use coarse, granulated table sugar, also known as crystal sugar, unless otherwise specified in our recipes.

sumac a purple-red, astringent spice ground from the berries of wild shrubs flourishing in the Mediterranean; adds a tart, lemony flavour to dips and dressings and goes well with barbecued meat. Can be found in Middle Eastern food stores.

tofu also known as bean curd or soybean curd; an off-white, custard-like product made from the "milk" of crushed soybeans. Refrigerate fresh tofu in water (changed daily) for up to 4 days.

firm tofu that has been compressed to remove most of the water. Used in stir-fries as it can be tossed without disintegrating.

fried packaged pieces of deep-fried soft tofu; the surface is brown and crunchy and the inside almost totally dried out. Add to soups and stir-fries at the last minute so they don't soak up too much liquid.

vinegar

balsamic originally from Modena, Italy, there are now many varieties on the market ranging in pungency and quality.

cider made from fermented apples.

malt made from fermented malt and beech shavings.

raspberry made from fresh raspberries steeped in a white wine vinegar.

red wine made from red wine.

rice also known as seasoned rice vinegar; a colourless vinegar made from fermented rice and flavoured with sugar and salt. Sherry can be substituted.

sherry natural vinegar aged in oak according to the traditional Spanish system; a mellow wine vinegar named for its colour.

tarragon white wine vinegar infused with fresh tarragon.

white wine made from white wine.

wasabi an Asian horseradish used to make the pungent, green-coloured sauce traditionally served with Japanese raw fish dishes; also sold in powdered or paste form.

white beans, canned a generic term we use for canned or dried cannellini, haricot, navy or great northern beans which are all of the same family – phaseolus vulgaris.

wombok also known as chinese cabbage or napa cabbage; elongated in shape with pale green, crinkly leaves.

yogurt we use plain full-cream yogurt in our recipes unless stated otherwise. If a recipe calls for low-fat yogurt, we use one with a fat content of less than 0.2 per cent.

zucchini also known as courgette.

index

conversion chart

MEASURES

One Australian metric measuring cup holds approximately 250ml, one Australian metric tablespoon holds 20ml, one Australian metric teaspoon holds 5ml.

The difference between one country's measuring cups and another's is within a two- or three-teaspoon variance, and will not affect your cooking results.North America, New Zealand and the United Kingdom use a 15ml tablespoon.

All cup and spoon measurements are level. The most accurate way of measuring dry ingredients is to weigh them. When measuring liquids, use a clear glass or plastic jug with the metric markings.

We use large eggs with an average weight of 60g.

LIQUID MEASURES

METRIC	IMPERIAL
30ml	1 fluid oz
60ml	2 fluid oz
100ml	3 fluid oz
125ml	4 fluid oz
150ml	5 fluid oz (¼ pint/1 gill)
190ml	6 fluid oz
250ml	8 fluid oz
300ml	10 fluid oz (½ pint)
500ml	16 fluid oz
600ml	20 fluid oz (1 pint)
1000ml (1 litre)	1¾ pints

LENGTH MEASURES

METRIC	IMPERIAL
3mm	⅛in
6mm	¼in
1cm	½in
2cm	¾in
2.5cm	1in
5cm	2in
6cm	2½in
8cm	3in
10cm	4in
13cm	5in
15cm	6in
18cm	7in
20cm	8in
23cm	9in
25cm	10in
28cm	11in
30cm	12in (1ft)

DRY MEASURES

METRIC	IMPERIAL
15g	½oz
30g	1oz
60g	2oz
90g	3oz
125g	4oz (¼lb)
155g	5oz
185g	6oz
220g	7oz
250g	8oz (½lb)
280g	9oz
315g	10oz
345g	11oz
375g	12oz (¾lb)
410g	13oz
440g	14oz
470g	15oz
500g	16oz (1lb)
750g	24oz (1½lb)
1kg	32oz (2lb)

OVEN TEMPERATURES

These oven temperatures are only a guide for conventional ovens.
For fan-forced ovens, check the manufacturer's manual.

	°C (CELSIUS)	°F (FAHRENHEIT)	GAS MARK
Very slow	120	250	½
Slow	150	275 – 300	1 – 2
Moderately slow	160	325	3
Moderate	180	350 – 375	4 – 5
Moderately hot	200	400	6
Hot	220	425 – 450	7 – 8
Very hot	240	475	9

Editorial director Susan Tomnay
Creative director Hieu Chi Nguyen
Food director Pamela Clark
Food editor Louise Patniotis
Senior editor Stephanie Kistner
Designer Caryl Wiggins
Nutrition information Rebecca Squadrito
Director of sales Brian Cearnes
Marketing manager Bridget Cody
Production manager Cedric Taylor

Chief executive officer Ian Law
Group publisher Pat Ingram
General manager Christine Whiston
Editorial director (WW) Deborah Thomas

WW food team Lyndey Milan, Alexandra Elliott, Frances Abdallaoui

Produced by ACP Books, Sydney.
Printing by Toppan Printing Co., Hong Kong
Published by ACP Magazines Ltd, 54 Park St, Sydney
GPO Box 4088, Sydney, NSW 2001
phone +61 2 9282 8618 fax +61 2 9267 9438
acpbooks@acpmagazines.com.au www.acpbooks.com.au
To order books phone 136 116 (within Australia)
Send recipe enquiries to recipeenquiries@acpmagazines.com.au

RIGHTS ENQUIRIES
Laura Bamford, Director ACP Books
lbamford@acpuk.com

Australia Distributed by Network Services,
phone +61 2 9282 8777 fax +61 2 9264 3278
networkweb@networkservicescompany.com.au
United Kingdom Distributed by Australian Consolidated Press (UK),
phone (01604) 497 531 fax (01604) 497 533
books@acpuk.com
Canada Distributed by Whitecap Books Ltd,
phone (604) 980 9852 fax (604) 980 8197
customerservice@whitecap.ca www.whitecap.ca
New Zealand Distributed by Netlink Distribution Company,
phone (9) 366 9966 ask@ndc.co.nz
South Africa Distributed by PSD Promotions,
phone (27 11) 392 6065/6/7 fax (27 11) 392 6079/80
orders@psdprom.co.za

Clark, Pamela.
The Australian Women's Weekly fast vegies.
ISBN 978-1-86396-595-8
1. Cookery (Vegetables). 2. Vegetarian cookery.
I. Title. II. Title: Australian women's weekly.
641.5636
© ACP Magazines Ltd 2007
ABN 18 053 273 546

Cover Grilled vegetable salad, page 363
Photographer Joshua Dasey
Stylist Justine Osborne
Food preparation Rebecca Squadrito
Additional photography Chris Chen
Acknowledgments Flemington Markets, Fratelli Fresh,
Vege King At The Entertainment Quarter Farmers Markets.